William S. Speer

Selections from the Encyclopedia of the New West

William S. Speer

Selections from the Encyclopedia of the New West

ISBN/EAN: 9783337222482

Printed in Europe, USA, Canada, Australia, Japan

Cover: Foto ©Andreas Hilbeck / pixelio.de

More available books at **www.hansebooks.com**

SELECTIONS FROM

THE

ENCYCLOPEDIA

OF

THE NEW WEST,

CONTAINING

FULLY AUTHENTICATED INFORMATION OF THE AGRICULTURAL, MERCANTILE,
COMMERCIAL, MANUFACTURING, MINING AND GRAZING INDUSTRIES,
AND REPRESENTING THE CHARACTER, DEVELOPMENT,
RESOURCES AND PRESENT CONDITION

OF

TEXAS, ARKANSAS, COLORADO, NEW MEXICO AND INDIAN TERRITORY.

ALSO,

BIOGRAPHICAL SKETCHES OF THEIR REPRESENTATIVE MEN AND WOMEN.

ILLUSTRATED WITH FINE STEEL PLATE PORTRAITS.

MARSHALL, TEXAS.
THE UNITED STATES BIOGRAPHICAL PUBLISHING COMPANY.
HODGE AND JENNINGS BROS., PROPRIETORS.

1881.

time since peace was established. His hand and purse are always open to worthy charities, and he gives cheerfully and liberally of his means to all public enterprises. Naturally modest and retiring in his disposition, when not occupied in business he prefers to enjoy the privacy of his comfortable and beautiful home and the society of his interesting family. He has never held a membership in any church, but with his wife is an attendant upon the Presbyterian, and contributes to its support. Their parents on both sides were Presbyterian in belief, and this is consequently the church of their choice, their children being always identified with the Sabbath school. Like his early ancestor, the famous Scottish "Wallace of Ellerslie," who lived nearly a thousand years ago, he is tall and handsome, weighing one hundred and twenty-five pounds. His eyes are dark gray and his hair black, though now thickly silvered with gray.

With a strong constitution, a firm will, temperate habits, good health and a cheerful temperament, he bids fair to be spared for many years of business, usefulness and happiness in the city where his lot is cast.

LEONARDO GARZA.

SAN ANTONIO.

LEONARDO GARZA was born in San Antonio, Texas, August 5, 1844. On the maternal side Mr. Garza is descended from the pioneer European family of San Antonio, he being a direct descendant of Maria Robaina de Betancur, the founder of the city. She was a native of the Canary Isles, and was treated with great distinction by the viceroy of Mexico, Juan de Acuna, Marquis de Casa-Fuerte, on her arrival on the American continent, on account of her distinguished lineage, she being a direct descendant of the renowned navigator, the Norman Baron Jean de Bethencourt, who conquered the Canary Isles in the year 1402. The present spelling of the name "Betancur," was adopted by the Baron's nephew, to accord to the Spanish tongue. On his paternal side, Mr. Garza traces his ancestors back to Brescia, in Lombardy, and an important river in that province was named in honor of the family. Some of the family went to Spain with Gonsalvo de Cordova, known as the Great Captain, after the end of the great battles in Italy, and from thence came to that portion of Mexico known as the New Philippines, or Las Texas, so named from an old Indian tribe. Geronimo de la Garza, his great-grandfather, came in the company of the thirteen families that settled San Antonio, and of whom "La Pobladora" de Betancur was the head. La Pobladora means original settler. The old homestead, partly built by him is still owned by the present Mr. Garza, and recently occupied by him as his place of residence. The old building is famous in Texas history, and was the first building taken by the American forces in the storming of Bexar. It is as strong as a fortress and will last for centuries yet. In this building was born Jose Antonio de la Garza, the father of the subject of this sketch, in the year 1777, and here he died in April, 1851.

He was a man of great influence in the county of Bexar, and was looked up to by the majority of the old settlers, by both the Spanish and Anglo-Americans. He was a man of considerable wealth, and gave employment to many persons. He was especially remarkable for his charities, and it was a common saying during his lifetime and after his death, "as charitable as old man Garza," or "tio Flacco," "Uncle Flacco," as he was familiarly called. In 1878 the legislature of Texas saw fit, in honor to his memory and to his family, to name one of the new counties for him. This was a merited compliment, for he did a great deal for the prosperity of San Antonio, for the county of Bexar, and for the great state of Texas.

Maria Josefa Menchaca, his wife, and mother of Leonardo Garza, was born in San Antonio, in 1805, in a house situated on the east side of Main Plaza and built by "La Pobladora" de Betancur, her great-great-grandmother. She was married at the early age of sixteen, and had many sons and daughters, of whom only one son is living and three daughters, the mother superior of the Ursuline Convent of San Antonio being one of them. She was a woman of remarkable strength of character and possessed an indomitable will. Left, while yet young, a widow with eight young children, she managed to educate them all, and at her death, which took place September 19, 1879, she left a competency for life for each and every one of her surviving children. She was well known in San Antonio and universally deplored, especially by the poor and needy, for she never turned a deaf ear to the call for charity. She was in word and deed a good mother and a worthy descendant of her illustrious maternal ancestor, Maria Robaina de Betancur.

Leonardo Garza was born in San Antonio, August 5, 1844. He remained in San Antonio up to his tenth year, when he was sent to Falmouth, Massachusetts, a town on Cape Cod, at that time quite unknown to fame, but lately become a famous watering place. Here is an old institution of learning known as Lawrence Academy, and here, after a five years' preparatory course, Mr. Garza graduated and then entered Williams College, in Williamstown, Berkshire county Massachusetts, in the class of 1864, but on account of the war between the North and South Mr. Garza did not graduate until 1865. During the whole civil war Mr. Garza did not receive news or letters from his relatives in Texas, and was obliged to get along the best way he could. At one time we find him in Philadelphia as teacher in St. Mark's Episcopal Academy, where he had under his charge the sons of the best families in Philadelphia, such as the McMichaels, Biddles, Pattersons, Godeys, Bishop Potter's son, Rusks, etc.; then again we find him in New York city canvassing for the great city directory, known as *Trow's City Directory*, but compiled at that time (1864) by Henry Wilson, in Greene street. Mr. Garza was employed by Mr. Wilson on *Wilson's Business and Copartnership Directory*. This was a lucrative position for Mr. Garza, but not being a permanent one, he left it to accept a position in the medical department of the United States navy, on board the double-ender "Patuxet." He remained in the service about five months, and resigned in February, 1865, re-entered college immediately, and graduated in the class of 1865. In November of the same year Mr. Garza returned to his native home in San Antonio, and was welcomed by his mother and relatives as one returned, as it were, from the dead, after an absence of eleven years from his native place.

During these years Mr. Garza enjoyed good health, and was kindly treated by the Northern people, for whom, during his long intercourse with them, he formed a strong attachment. For him there is no North, no South—but one country, now and forever.

In the year of the great exposition in Paris, 1867, Mr. Garza made a trip to Europe and remained away one year. While in Europe he saw many things to admire and which he deemed worthy of imitation in this country, but nevertheless, on the whole, he was inclined to say: "Give me my native country in preference to all others." As between France, England and Germany, he preferred France, and is well satisfied in his own mind that the French people are the most prosperous and happy of all Europeans. Some six months after his return from abroad, that

is, in June, 1868, he was married to Miss Caroline Callaghan, daughter of the late Bryan Callaghan and C. Ramon de Callaghan.

Mr. Callaghan was born in the city of Cork, Ireland, and was a gentleman highly esteemed in San Antonio, and one of the most influential that ever lived in Bexar. While mayor of San Antonio, he did a great deal for the improvement of the city and his administration is praised even to this day. Mr. Callaghan died in 1854 at the early age of forty-two, being at that time the most prosperous merchant and wealthiest man in the city. He died beloved by all and was universally mourned.

His wife, Miss C. Ramon, is a native of San Antonio, and a descendent of the first families that settled the place. She is still living, and resides in the city. Mrs. Caroline C. Garza was born in San Antonio in June, 1850, was married June, 1868. Her first child, Josephine, was born in July, 1870; Leonard born in October, 1872; Francis, born in February, 1874, and died in September, 1874; Bryan, born in December, 1875; Rudolph, born in April, 1878.

Both Mr. Garza and his wife are Catholics. He is a Democrat in politics. He never held office; belongs to no society of any kind; is now engaged in the real estate business and is president of the Occidental Land Company, a corporation duly chartered under the laws of Texas "for the purpose of preparing and keeping a perfect and complete abstract of all the land titles in Bexar county and other counties of western Texas—to furnish chains of title to any lands in Bexar and other counties of western Texas to such persons as may apply for them—to buy and sell lands for the benefit of the company, or for other persons on commission—to pay taxes for residents or non-residents, and to do a general real estate business."

HERMANN MARWITZ.

GALVESTON.

ARRIVING in Galveston, Texas, in 1851, with fifty dollars in his pocket; in 1860 beginning business as a retail grocer with a capital of $1000, Mr. Marwitz is now senior member in the firm of H. Marwitz & Co., wholesale and retail grocers and ship-chandlers, corner of Mechanic and Twenty-third streets, in which he has $40,000 invested, the annual sales amounting to $120,000. The junior partner is Mr. F. W. Miller, who was his clerk from 1868 to 1876, when he became a partner with one-half interest in the business.

As further evidence of his prosperity, Mr. Marwitz owns a residence which cost him $15,000, five improved places, and several unimproved lots in the city. How did he make his fortune? He answers: "By doing whatever I could find to do, until by hard licks and economy I had made enough to go into trade"—a field open to all in this land.

Mr. Marwitz was born in Magdeburg, Prussia, September 30, 1831. His father, Mr. G. Marwitz, was a manufacturer of crockery, who died in 1848. Most of his relatives still reside in Europe, engaged in various industrial pursuits. His mother, Mrs. Louise Marwitz, died in Galveston at the age of seventy-eight. She was the daughter of Mr. Patte, a descendant of the French Huguenots who fled from persecution in 1685.

Mr. Marwitz had a fair common school education at Magdeburg. After leaving school, he served five years as an apprentice to the grocer's business, and then, as said before, he came to Galveston in 1851, when its population was from five to six thousand. He had the good fortune to marry, in 1859, Miss Bertha Plitt, born in Hessen, Germany, July 9, 1840, daughter of George Plitt, who died in two weeks after his arrival, leaving a wife and five children. Bertha was the youngest of the five. Mr. and Mrs. Marwitz have but one child, Ida Mary, born in Galveston, January 10, 1864, and educated at the Ursuline Convent, Galveston. Mr. Marwitz, in 1861, when the war began, enlisted in the Galveston Sappers and Miners, an engineer corps in which he continued until 1864, and (he says) as he only handled wheelbarrows, he never killed a man on either side.

Mr. Marwitz belongs to the Lutheran church. In politics he is independent. He is a member of the German society for the purpose of building up German schools and churches and assisting emigrants to get a start in business on these hospitable shores. He is a member of the Garten Verein and Casino, both German societies formed for amusement after working hours. The former is a very select and aristocratic society. Its garden is hardly excelled by the parks of San Antonio. Mr. Marwitz is in person the true type of the German, and has the air of a successful business gentleman.

AUGUSTUS C. ALLEN.

HOUSTON.

THIS gentleman, well known in the earlier days of Texas, was born at Saratoga, New York, on the 4th day of July, 1806. He grew up and was educated in Oneida county, and for some time afterwards was professor of mathematics in the Polytechnic Institute at Chatenango. From there he went to New York City and become interested for several years in a banking house. He subsequently followed merchandising in Baldwinville, New York, until he moval to Nacogdoches, Texas, in 1833. At Baldwinville, on the 3d of May, 1831, he married Charlotte M., daughter of Dr. Jonas C. Baldwin, the founder of that town. She was born in Onandaga county, on the 14th of July, 1805, nearly a year prior to the birth of her husband, and came with him to Texas in 1833. Mr. Allen removed from Nacogdoches, in company with his brother, John K., soon after the battle of San Jacinto, to Buffalo bayou, where they bought and settled on the land upon which the city of Houston stands. Under the firm name of A. C. & J. K. Allen, they laid out a town site, on a liberal scale, and made propositions to the first congress of Texas, assembled at Columbia, in October, 1836, for the location of the seat of government at that place, to be called Houston, in honor of the newly inaugurated president. Their proposals were accepted and, early in 1837, the government was removed there. They built, of their own means, the first capitol of the republic, as a donation; which, however, reverted to them on the removal of the seat of government from Houston to Austin, in 1839. They donated lots for churches, schools, etc., and in every way manifested a liberal spirit in building up the town. They were known all over Texas as men of energy and enterprise, combined with business sagacity and liberal views. The fine city of to-day is a monument to their early conceptions. Their brothers, Samuel and Harvey H. Allen, also became well-known citizens of Houston. A. C. Allen, was also a share-holder in the stock of the Galveston City Company; a large operator in lands, with handsome profits, and in various ways connected with enterprises to build up the country. Though never officially connected with them, he was an early friend and contributor to the infantile railroad

enterprises projected from Houston as the initial point. Mr. Allen and Mosley Baker were the originators of the Houston and Texas Central railway.

About the year 1852 he was appointed United States Consul at the Mexican ports of Minatitlan, on the Gulf, and Tahuantepec on the Pacific, the termini of an isthmus route, then engaging the public mind and now (1884) almost a perfected fact. He remained there about ten years, and, with Mr. Welsh, an Englishman, established a trade from Minatitlan to Europe, through a line of sail vessels; shipping largely and profitably vanilla, cochineal, dye-woods and mahogany. After the war between the states began, Mr. Allen, repaired to New York, to settle his accounts with the government, resign his office, make that city his future home and engage in banking. His health, however, had been declining for two or three years, causing him to travel extensively in the West Indies and elsewhere. His wife was in Texas and he sent for her to join him in New York. She could only do so by going to Matamoros, on account of the blockade, and a little before she reached him, he breathed his last. She arrived in time, however, to see his remains deposited in the beautiful cemetery of Greenwood, Brooklyn, in the soil of his native state, after an absence of thirty years.

Mr. Allen was a small man, full of energy, directed by a clear head, and possessed those qualities which win and hold friends. He was an especial friend of General Houston and had kindly relations with most of the public men of Texas.

Mrs. Allen, yet residing in Houston, at the age of seventy-six, justly ranks as one of the mothers of Texas; having come in her early womanhood, before the revolution of 1835, and remained its steadfast friend for forty-eight years. Endowed with those traits which adorn womankind, blessed with an early education, from her first location in Nacogdoches to her palatial home of to-day, she has been endeared to her people as one altogether deserving their love and respect. Very fitly she may be styled the mother of the city of Houston, with twenty thousand people, railroads, steam-boats, factories and mansions, for she has nursed it, watched it and been of it from its first log but to its present position. Honored be the memory of such a mother.

Mr. and Mrs. Allen had four children, three of whom died in infancy or childhood. The only survivor is their daughter Martha E. W., the wife of Mr. James Converse, civil engineer, to whom she was married on the 21st of September, 1873. She is an accomplished and estimable lady, and has only one child, Thomas Pierce Converse, born July 11, 1876. These two are the only living offspring of A. C. Allen.

Mr. Converse was born in Aurora, Ohio, on the 21st of September, 1828, and received a liberal education, including civil engineering. He has been identified with the interests of Houston for many years and with the Galveston, Harrisburg and San Antonio railway, almost from its inception, and is now its general superintendent. He has energy, intelligence and integrity, and has been a valuable factor in the progress of that great work, still wending its way, as its pet name indicates, towards the "sun-set."

JUDGE NAT. M. BURFORD.

DALLAS.

NAT. M. BURFORD was born in Smith county, Tennessee, on the 24th day of June, (St. John's day,) 1824. His father was John Hawkins Burford, a native of North Carolina, of English descent. His mother was Nancy McAlister, a Virginia girl of Welsh extraction. His grandfathers, on both sides, were Revolutionary soldiers. His father was a soldier under General Andrew Jackson in the war of 1812-15, but after that he led the quiet life of an independent farmer in Smith county, Tennessee, where his children were born and reared. He died at the age of seventy-five, and his wife at the age of eighty. They were highly respected in all the surrounding country, and were among those old Tennessee families personally known to and loved by General Jackson. Of their children only five are living—three daughters and two sons. The daughters are the mothers of families and still reside in Tennessee. William C., one of the sons, was a soldier in the Mexican war and wounded at the battle of Cerro Gordo. He was also a major and a gallant soldier in the Confederate army. Never having married, he lives a quiet life in Tarrant county, Texas.

Nathaniel Macon Burford, the subject of this sketch, named in honor of the greatest statesman North Carolina ever produced, and as pure and patriotic a man as ever sat in the councils of the New World, was denied the advantages of collegiate education, his father being unable to furnish the same, but at the age of seventeen, by teaching country schools, he was enabled to pass through a course of study at Irving College, in which trying process he passed three years. He then studied law in the office of the Hon. A. J. Marchbanks, in McMinnville, Tennessee, and was licensed as a lawyer by his preceptor, then on the bench, and Chancellor Broomfield Ridley, in October, 1845. For a time he located at Jasper, in East Tennessee, and had fine prospects of success, but he soon became restless and desirous of adventure in new fields. He volunteered as a soldier for the Mexican war, but when his company reached Knoxville, the quota of the state had been filled. The services of the company were declined, but young Burford, desirous of serving the cause, presented his horse, a noble animal, to Dr. John T. Reed, a surgeon in a regiment already mustered in. For a moment he returned to Jasper, but in December, 1846, started for the great Southwest.

Short of funds, he worked his way, as a deck passenger, to Shreveport, Louisiana, where he arrived with an actual and live capital of two dollars and fifty cents. He walked on foot to Jefferson, Texas, where he at once obtained the position of deputy clerk of the district court under Willis H. Childress, as noble a man as ever hailed from North Alabama. The bar was too full to encourage his aspirations, and after a considerable service, replenished in purse, he rode into the hamlet of Dallas on the 1st day of October, 1848, astride of a twenty-five dollar pony, his own property, with five dollars in his pocket, and numerous letters of recommendation to several of the twelve adult males then composing its sovereignty. He filed his homestead claim on the town, by posting his shingle as a lawyer, speedily formed a law partnership with John H. Reagan, whose name is now national, and rapidly grew in practice. A thorough, but most liberal and generous Democrat, he soon became a favorite in this then Democratic community. In 1850, and again in 1852, he was elected prosecuting attorney of the district in which Dallas was, covering an immense territory. He won great popular favor as a faithful and successful prosecutor, but utterly refused to lend countenance to malicious or vindictive actions, trampling them under foot as vile and detestable, and thus elevated, in public esteem, the judiciary of the state.

By a law of 1856, the sixteenth judicial district was created, embracing the counties of Ellis, Dallas, Collin, Grayson, and all the counties and territory west of them. He was elected judge of this new district. He, therefore, held the first court in several counties of the west, as Johnson, Parker, Palo Pinto, Wise, Young, Jack, Clay, etc.

When the war came in the spring of 1861, he enlisted as a private in the 1st Texas artillery company, commanded by his townsman, John J. Good. He served in this battery till the winter of 1861-2; but in that time his commanding officer, General Ben

C. L. Cleveland

McCulloch, who knew his worth, went to Richmond, and he, in conjunction with John H. Reagan, then postmaster-general of the Confederate States, and a former partner of Judge Burford, secured for him a commission to raise a regiment. The regiment was speedily raised, in the spring of 1862, and mustered into the Confederate service as the 19th Texas cavalry. But, though holding a commission as its colonel, he refused to serve until the same was ratified by a vote of the regiment, which was done unanimously.

The entire service of the regiment was confined to the Trans-Mississippi department in Arkansas, Louisiana and Texas. Among the engagements in which it participated, while under command of Colonel Burford, were the battles of Mansfield, Blair's Landing, and Monett's Ferry. He was almost in touching distance of the noble and fearless General Tom Green, when he was killed at Blair's Landing.

Prompted by ill-health, he resigned his commission in September, 1864, and returned home.

In 1866, under President Johnson's reconstruction proclamation, he was elected to the legislature from Dallas county, and by the house of representatives, when assembled, he was elected speaker.

In April, 1875, he was elected presiding justice of Dallas county, and in February, 1876, (under the new constitution,) was elected judge of the eleventh judicial district, composed of the populous counties of Dallas and Ellis. In July, 1877, against the protest of many friends, he resigned this position. On the creation of north Texas, in 1879, as a distinct district of the United States judicial system, though an unchanged Democrat, he was appointed a United States commissioner, resident in Dallas, which position he now holds, honorably and acceptably.

On the 18th of January, 1854, Judge Burford married Mary J., daughter of O. B. Knight, a pioneer of Dallas county. With this excellent and universally esteemed lady, his married life has been singularly blessed in domestic felicity. Of eight children, five still survive under the parental roof, viz: Mattie, a very lovely young woman, (this by the editor, who knows her well and tenderly esteems her,) born February 16, 1861; Nathaniel M. jr., born August 20, 1866; Robert Lee, born in 1870; Jeff. Mallard, born in 1876, and Mary J., born in September, 1879. Mrs. Burford is one of those rare women, reared in the wilderness, to whom chivalry and manhood bow, whether in the hut or the palace, and hence she is a pet with all the old pioneers of Dallas county, who have known her as child, girl, woman, mother and wife. The compiler of this rude sketch of the husband would be derelict to his sense of manhood not to pay this tribute to so pure and so good a woman as Mary Knight Burford. It is a sincere tribute to meritorious worth.

Mrs. Burford is a Southern Methodist, while the Judge is an Episcopalian—neither tainted with that clanish bigotry which so often mars otherwise loveable characters.

Judge Burford is yet but in the full tide of manhood—only fifty-six years of age—and may yet do good service to his country. He is an affable, genial man, generous to his own detriment—a fine conversationalist, fond of polite and biographic literature, and though not a poet, has much of poetry in his nature. He exemplifies, strikingly, a quaint saying of the Southwest, embodying the superlative idea of nobility in nature, in the expression, " He has a heart as big as a mountain!" He is a type of early men in north Texas, steadily passing away, whose individual labors are doomed to oblivion, but whose aggregate will be immortalized in the ultimate grandeur of this peerless region of the Southwest.

JUDGE CHARLES LANDER CLEVELAND.

GALVESTON.

CHARLES L. CLEVELAND was born in Breckenridge county, Kentucky, August 25, 1824. He is the son of Jesse A. H. Cleveland, who was born in Virginia, moved with his father to Kentucky, married Sarah Lander in Fayette county, was a farmer, a man of first-rate English education, a superior mathematician, in early life engaged in surveying in Kentucky, and moved from that state to Memphis, Tennessee, in 1831; in 1833 moved to Brazoria county, Texas, when his wife died, the first victim of cholera in that state; followed merchandising in Brazoria two years, settled on a farm near Barnard river in 1835, was a soldier under General Houston in 1836, moved to Galveston in 1841, having a considerable fortune, consisting principally of slaves; was deputy United States marshal under General Ben McCulloch during the latter's term, and had entire control of the office. In 1844 Jesse A. H. Cleveland, without pretending to any knowledge of the theory or practice of medicine, while the yellow fever was raging in Galveston, undertook the cure of that disease and was wonderfully successful, insomuch that he continued to treat patients afflicted with the disease for years afterward. He probably met with better success than any man in the South. The method of cure, without medicine, was published in the papers and periodicals, and proved to be more successful than any other mode of treatment ever adopted. He treated more than five hundred cases. His diagnosis and treatment were unfailing, and his method is known as the "Cleveland Treatment." Thousands in Galveston well remember Jesse A. H. Cleveland in connection with yellow fever, as he attended them night and day when afflicted with the plague. He was a man of great firmness and decision of character, and noted for his boundless generosity and hospitality. He died in Galveston in 1876.

Jesse Cleveland, the paternal grandfather of Charles L. Cleveland, was born at Mount Vernon, Virginia, was a man of strongly-marked personal characteristics, and died in extreme old age, at Galesburg, Illinois. His mother, Sarah Lander, was a native of Fayette county, Kentucky, and died at Brazoria, Texas, in 1833.

Charles L. Cleveland was a farmer's boy till the age of thirteen, when he entered the office of the Texas *Republican*, in Brazoria, Texas, which was worked on the first press ever introduced into Texas. It was known as the "war organ." While engaged on this paper Colonel William H. Jack, who is known in Texas history, was a contributor. Mr. Cleveland became well acquainted with him, and says of him that he was a most persuasive, silver-tongued, magnetic orator, a lawyer who stood in the front rank of the Texas bar, a speaker who carried a jury, court, or crowd with equal facility; the author of the Turtle bayou resolutions that bear the same relation to the Texas declaration of independence that the Mecklenburg resolutions bear to the Colonial Declaration of Independence. They were written on Turtle bayou with a pen made from a cane cut from its banks.

Mr. Cleveland also worked in the office of the *Telegraph*, a paper published at Columbia, on the Brazos, then the seat of government of the republic of Texas. Having worked several months in that office, he entered Rutersville College in Fayette county, from which institution he graduated with the degree of master of arts in 1842. The same year he went to Galveston, whither his father had moved in 1841 from Brazoria, and began the study of law, his preceptor being Judge Benjamin C. Franklin. He was admitted to the bar at Liberty in 1846. He remained at Liberty, and for twenty-five years devoted himself to the practice of his profession there. That he met with encouragement and pecuniary as well as professional success, may readily be inferred when it is stated that he began his career without means, having only his profession and an honorable ambition, and that he is now the owner of a large and valuable property. In June, 1871, he formed a partnership with Judge Willie, of Galveston, to which city he removed, and where he now resides. The business of the firm is very extensive, and no lawyers rank higher than they at the Galveston bar.

From Liberty county Mr. Cleveland was elected to serve in the sixth legislature of Texas, and served one term, Governor Pease being then the chief executive of the state. Major John Henry Brown characterizes his career in the legislature as especially useful in checking hasty, inconsiderate and injudicious action, and more distinguished for preventing bad legislation than for the introduction of original measures. August, 1860, he was elected Judge of the first judicial district of Texas, and this position he held until removed by Provisional Governor Hamilton, in 1865. No civil officers of the state were allowed to remain in office unless they would take and subscribe to the iron-clad oath. Those refusing to submit to this test of loyalty were regarded as impediments to reconstruction, and were accordingly removed. In 1861, while he was judge, he was elected a delegate to the secession convention from Liberty and Polk counties. The convention assembled in January, 1861. Judge Cleveland advocated and voted for the ordinance of secession, urging its submission to the people, by whom it was subsequently ratified by a vote of four to one. This important statement of a historical fact will correct the impression that the convention favored the adoption of the ordinance of secession, and the withdrawal of the state from the Union without the concurrence of the people as expressed at the ballot-box. Judge Cleveland supported secession and the war with all his influence and energy. He was a delegate to the Democratic state convention in 1857 from Liberty county, and in 1873 and 1876 from Galveston.

Charles L. Cleveland and Mrs. Mary Ann Booker were married April 9, 1849, in Liberty county, Texas. She is the daughter of Benjamin Watson Hardin, one of the pioneers of Texas, from Maury county, Tennessee. She was born January 5, 1829, in Liberty county, Texas, and was educated in Galveston. Her father and his three brothers, William, Augustine Blackburn and Franklin Hardin moved to Texas in 1828. William was primary judge of the jurisdiction of Liberty, department of Nacogdoches, from 1833 to 1836; was one of the eleven founders and original proprietors of the league of land upon which the city of Galveston was established, was associated with M. B. Menard in the organization of the Galveston City Company, and died in Galveston in 1838. Augustine Blackburn Hardin was a member of the "Consultation," which convened at San Felipe in 1835, and established a provisional government for Texas before its final separation from Mexico; was a soldier of the Texas revolution, and a member of the company commanded by his brother Franklin, and died in Liberty in 1871. Franklin Hardin was the first surveyor of the Liberty land district, entered the army in 1836 as a lieutenant in Captain Logan's company, and participated in the battle of San Jacinto; in the fall of 1836 organized and commanded a company in the army under General Rusk, and continued in the service until the close of the revolution; was elected to the state legislature in 1858 from Liberty county; died April 20, 1859, and was buried on the anniversary of the battle of San Jacinto, of which he was one of the heroes. Benjamin W. Hardin, father of Mrs. Cleveland, was a member of the *Ayuntiemento* of the jurisdiction of Liberty, under the government of Mexico, and subsequently under the republic of Texas; held the office of sheriff several terms—a resolute man of great personal courage and unquestionable integrity, distinguished for hospitality, kindness and benevolence. He died in Liberty county, January 2, 1849.

From the marriage of Judge Cleveland and his wife nine children have been born: Watson H.

born March 16, 1850, died July 18, 1867 ; Stewart, born September 24, 1852, died March 17, 1854 ; John Stewart, born December 18, 1854 ; Lander, born March 17, 1857 ; Oliver, born December 16, 1859 ; Sarah, born November 26, 1862, died July 12, 1864 ; Charles Sidney, born September 16, 1865 ; Jesse W., born March 31, 1869 ; Willie F., born March 3, 1872.

Judge Cleveland and his wife are both members of the Methodist Episcopal Church South, but their children who belong to any religious society are members of the Baptist church. Judge Cleveland adheres to the Methodist tenets because of the broad and liberal grounds they occupy, while he accepts orthodox Christianity in every guise, and looks more to the life of the individual than to the particular creed or theory of church government he may espouse. His political principles are characteristically Democratic. Judge Cleveland became a Mason in 1848, in Liberty Lodge No. 48, and was master of that lodge for sixteen years. He has also taken the Royal Arch degrees. He was deputy district grand master for the first judicial district for several years.

Judge Cleveland's possessions are extensive. On the corner of Church and Twelfth streets, Galveston, he owns a residence valued at $4,000. Two other dwelling houses in the city belonging to him are worth $6,000. Besides these possessions, he has in fee simple 50,000 acres of land, unimproved, in Bastrop, Bexar, Blanco, Bosque, Brown, Burnet, Callahan, Chambers, Clay, Coleman, Comanche, Denton,

Hardin, Jefferson, Karnes, Liberty, Montgomery, Polk, San Jacinto, Taylor, Travis, Tyler and Williamson counties. He is a director of the Texas Banking and Insurance Company, and also a stockholder. He is a stockholder in the Gulf Loan and Homestead Company, the Southern Cotton Compress Company, the Texas Cotton Press and Manufacturing Company, and the Galveston Gas Company, and is vice president of the Island City Protestant Orphans' Home.

During all his business life Judge Cleveland has given his special attention to the minutest details of his affairs. His success consists not so much in large receipts, as in taking care of what he has made. Frugal and unostentatious in life and bearing, he is warm in his attachments, generous and benevolent. His surplus earnings he invested judiciously from time to time, in lands. He has been scrupulously exact in meeting his obligations, and no note of his ever went to protest. His credit has always been good, because he never strained it, nor subjected it to hazard. He avoided contracting a debt without seeing how it could be paid at maturity, and paying it promptly.

Judge Cleveland is a first-class man, whether we regard him as a civilian, a lawyer, or business man. His position is an enviable one, and it has been reached not by any improper arts, but by industry, integrity, the exercise of sound judgment, and the employment of the highest principles known to enlightened society.

JAMES BOYLE.

SHERMAN.

MR. BOYLE, though seventy-four years of age, has the erect figure, the elastic step and easy carriage of a well preserved gentleman. He has evidently studied, read, thought, traveled, observed, written and conversed much during all these years, so that their results have become a part of the man's personal presence, impressing themselves most agreeably upon every one who is so fortunate as to be thrown into his company. Mr. Boyle is of Quaker and Irish ancestry. His grandfather, Connel O'Boyle, was a sea captain, and a descendant of the O'Badhues, a race of Irish Kings. He married Miss Alice Dugan, in Donegal, Ireland, immigrated to this country and settled in Philadelphia, when John, the father of Mr. James Boyle, who was born in 1781, was yet an infant.

John Boyle, when eighteen years of age, became a member of McCarthy's surveying party, passing through Zanesville, Ohio, where there was but one house, a log cabin, in the place. Going afterwards to Delaware, he attended school in Mill Creek Hundred, a Quaker settlement eight miles north of Wilmington. Here he became acquainted with a charming young Quakeress, whom he shortly after married.

After the birth of four children, one son, (James,) and three daughters, they removed to Ohio, and settled on a farm near Zanesville, where he died in the seventy-fourth year of his age, a few years after the death of his wife.

James Boyle, born in Delaware in 1806, passed his childhood from three years old to twelve in the school room, and from that time till he was twenty in working on his father's farm. Going to Illinois, he attended Rock Spring Seminary for a time, then returned to Ohio and finished his course of study in the colleges of Kenyon and Granville. He was then for nine years county surveyor of Muskingum county. He next entered the Law School of Cincinnati and graduated in 1837. Removing from Zanesville to Cincinnati, he practiced his profession in that city thirty years, gaining prominence in his profession, and the confidence of all the leading men of the city.

Mr. Boyle married the youngest daughter of Colonel George Jackson, the hero of three wars—those of the Revolution, Indian and the war of 1812. He was a member of congress, first from Virginia, afterwards from Ohio. Stonewall Jackson and William L. Jackson, both well known names, were of the same family. The eldest son of Mr. George Jackson succeeded him in congress. He became brother-in-law to James Madison, and his youngest son, Andrew R. Jackson, was a member of the California legislature. By his marriage with Miss Jackson, Mr. Boyle had eight children, five sons and three daughters. The oldest, John G., is married, has one child, and is United States district attorney, having his residence in Galveston; Carrol Gleason has a wife and one child, was civil engineer on the Texas and Pacific railway, but is now in Chicago in the varnish business; George Jackson is married, and was civil engineer on the Texas and Pacific, but is now yardmaster for the same company at Sherman; Frank White is married and has been a clerk in the United States custom house in Galveston since 1874; Percy, the youngest, is assistant yardmaster at Sherman. Of the daughters. Louise, is the wife of Watts De Golyer, a varnish maker at Riverside, near Chicago; Lucy G. is the wife of Edward Cook, a ship chandler of Chicago, and Helen, the youngest daughter, is still unmarried and with her parents.

In 1874 Mr. Boyle left Cincinnati and moved to Galveston. Four of his sons had preceded him to Texas. In 1876 he removed to Sherman, where he lived, admired by many and honored by all. As a writer he has sought more to amuse himself than to achieve fame. Some of the productions of his pen have, however, been given to the public. Among them should be particularly mentioned his abridged translation of *Quintilian's Institutiones Oratoriae*, a work of no inconsiderable labor, but performed with great correctness and fidelity to the original, and receiving the commendation of men of learning as a masterly production.

Mr. Boyle has but one sister living, Isabel, the wife of Rev. William Porter, presiding elder of the Methodist Episcopal church of Zanesville, Ohio. He (Mr. Boyle) is, in politics, independent of party; is a member of the Christian church, ever ready at the call of duty, with a liberal response either in charity or sympathy.

Mrs. Boyle is a lady not unknown to fame. Many leading papers and magazines have been enriched by her poetic contributions, and though as wife and mother of a large family she has excelled, she has found time to indulge her taste for literature. Such are the women whose names deserve to be chronicled among the noble ones of our country.

DR. M. A. CORNELIUS.

DALLAS.

IN JULY, 1872, Dr. Cornelius came to Dallas on borrowed money, and has acquired a good practice, a good home, and the confidence of a large portion of a very mixed and new community in his skill as a physician and his reputation as a gentleman.

Dr. Cornelius was born near Huntsville, Madison county, Alabama, January 2, 1832, and raised on a farm. Besides the ordinary schools of that country, he had the advantage of four years' attendance at the McKenzie Institute, under the celebrated Dr. John W. P. McKenzie, of Red River county, Texas, and afterwards of taking private lessons in Latin, mathematics and several of the sciences under Mr. Teasdale, in Henderson, Texas.

His father, Absalom Cornelius, was born in South Carolina, moved first to Wilkes county, Georgia, where he married, thence to Alabama, and in 1838 to Texas, where he died in 1845. His mother, Margaret Ward, was the daughter of Matt Ward, an Irishman, a farmer and slaveholder in Talladega county, Alabama. She died at the house of her son in Dallas, at the age of eighty-six. Her brothers were Colonel Matt Ward, for years a member of the Texas congress and United States senator before the war commenced, Martin, Thomas J., Dr. William, John and Lewis Ward, all good and solid men. Dr. William Ward, a banker and railroad man at Jefferson, Texas, (whose daughter, Mary Ward, was married to Judge John L. Camp, of Gilmer, Texas.) Professor Sam Ward, of Jefferson, and Rev. William E. Ward, once editor of the *Banner of Peace* and founder of Ward Seminary, Nashville, are her nephews.

Dr. Cornelius has two brothers living: Roland Cornelius, an independent farmer at Henderson, Texas, married to Martha Dyer, daughter of General John Dyer, of Red River county; Captain W. P. Cornelius, farmer and merchant, Clarksville, Texas, who has been three times married—first to Arabella, daughter of Edward West, for many years sheriff of Red River county; next, to Mrs. Reagan, a widowed daughter of Mrs. Mary Donahoe, and lastly, to Mrs. Herbert.

Four of the Doctor's brothers are dead: Ira, Hiram, Martin D., John L. and Thomas J. These were all men grown and had been successful in business. His living sisters are Mary Tullora, first married to George W. Dyer, a farmer, in the year 1846, and next to Ross Powell, of Cass county. They now live in Red River county. She has one son, Robert Dyer, a farmer near Waco, and Caledonia A., a daughter, now the wife of Colonel William A. Shaw, a lawyer and planter on Red river. He was a member for that county in the Texas legislature in 1873.

Dr. Cornelius was destined by his father for a lawyer. Accordingly he commenced reading in the office of Armstrong & McClarty, Henderson, Texas, but soon abandoned it for the study of medicine, and commenced reading with his brother, Dr. Martin D

daughter of James Driskell, a stock-dealer of Sanga-
mon county. After his marriage he went on his farm,
in Logan county, where he remained five years, doing
a profitable business.

His wife's health proving delicate, he conceived
the design of removing to Texas. In doing so he
rejected the example of his uncles on both sides, and
was the first of the family to strike out alone on the
great sea of business. In 1872 he leased his farm
and removed to Fort Worth, Texas.

Mr. and Mrs. Lake have three children: Ollie M.,
born October 18, 1871; Thomas W., born July 30,
1874, and James Wilham, born January 20, 1876.

Mr. Lake is not a politician, nor does he take an
interest in political affairs, but generally votes with
the Republicans. He is a member of the Knights of
Pythias. Neither he nor his wife is a member of any
religious society, but both contribute liberally to
church enterprises and the support of the ministry.
He has always been a man of steady habits, and
indulges in no form of dissipation.

In November, 1875, with a capital of $2,000, he
began the hardware business in Fort Worth. During
the first year his sales amounted to $35,000. The
next year they reached $60,000, and they steadily
increased, until in the year 1879 they amounted to
$85,000, and he estimates his sales for the year 1880
at $100,000.

His business house is located on the corner of Second and Houston streets. The main building is
fifty by one hundred feet in size, and is the property
of Mr. Lake. He has three warehouses: one near the
depot, in which he stores agricultural implements; one
in the south part of town, used for stores, and a third
on Third street, for storing tinners' stock, nails, sheet-
iron, wire, etc. His wholesale trade extends into all
the counties of western Texas that are tributary to
Fort Worth. Besides the store and warehouses previously mentioned, he owns a private residence
worth $2,500, a farm of one hundred and sixty acres
in Tarrant county, several hundred acres of wild land
in Dickinson county, and a farm of one hundred and
sixty acres in Logan county, Illinois. He owns a
small interest in the El Paso hotel, and has other
interests of minor value.

His success is attributable solely to close attention
to business from early morning till late at night. He
is not afraid to take hold of any hard work necessary
to be done. He treats all customers with courtesy,
keeps his word and stands up to his agreements, and
sees that his men, of whom he employs about ten,
do the same.

JOHN JAY GOOD.

DALLAS.

AMONG the men of note who entered manhood's
struggle in north Texas, stands forth John Jay
Good, of Dallas, the son of a worthy and prosperous manufacturer at Columbus, Mississippi, who gave
him a good education in the primaries of the country
and at Cumberland College, Lebanon, Tennessee.
When just entering manhood's estate, he settled as a
lawyer in the village of Dallas, Texas, and has ever
since resided there, and is now (1881) the mayor of
the then village, but now a prosperous city of fifteen
thousand inhabitants.

He soon married Susan A., daughter of Mr. Nat C.
Floyd, from Union county, Kentucky, a lady of
refinement and great excellence of character, yet
spared to him, by whom he has six children, the eldest
of whom is his present law partner.

As a lawyer his standing has ever been honorable,
in both civil and criminal business. He has never
sought to make a specialty of either, but rather to be a
useful lawyer to his fellow citizens whose necessities
demanded the employment of such. When young
he imbibed a love of military life, and while a mere
boy was elected a general of militia in Alabama, hence
was early styled General Good, but had too much of
the leaven of common sense to esteem such a title, so
held, as of intrinsic value in the estimation of character.

From his location in Dallas in 1851 to this year of
1881, he has been a consistent Democrat, often on the

stump, and always at war with centralism and those
tendencies which he believed pointed towards a cen-
tralized government; in other words, a monarchy to
be erected on the ruins of free government. For
thirty years, in season and out of season, he has been
a faithful sentinel on the watch-tower of public liberty.

When Mr. Lincoln was elected as a sectional president in 1860, Mr. Good was an open and avowed
advocate of secession, and made many addresses to
the people in favor of the measure. He organized
and was elected captain of the first artillery company
in Texas offered to the Confederate government. As
such he was under General Ben McCulloch, in
southwest Missouri, in the fall of 1861, and performed
gallant deeds at Elkhorn in March, 1862. Transferred to the east side of the Mississippi immediately
afterwards, his battery did gallant service in the battle
of Farmington, following that of Shiloh and preceding
the bloody day at Corinth. About that time a reorganization of the army occurred, and Captain Good
returned to his home in Dallas, but soon after joined
a regiment newly organized and commanded by
Colonel B. Warren Stone; but he soon received a
commission appointing him presiding justice of a
standing military court east of the Mississippi, with the
military rank of colonel. He at once repaired to his
new field of duty, and there continued till the close of
the war, when, with his family, he returned to Dallas in

18-T

1865 utterly broken up and with only twenty dollars in money. As a military judge, it is said his rulings were always on the side of personal liberty and against the despotic exercise of power.

On the reorganization of the state in 1866, he was elected district judge, by a large majority of the district in which he lived, embracing eleven counties. His administration was acceptable to the people, but in 1867 he was driven from the bench, as "an impediment to reconstruction," by the order of a military satrap then stationed in New Orleans as a ruler over Louisiana and Texas. The name of this satrap, strutting in a little brief authority and drunken with pompous self-conceit, was Philip H. Sheridan, the same who deposed Throckmorton, the people's chosen governor, and appointed in his stead a man who had been rejected by the people at the polls by a vote of more than four to one. As naturally as honor detests meanness, these actions, followed by a second and forced system of reconstruction, wherein the intelligence and virtue of the state were largely denied a voice, and enfranchised ignorance was placed in the ascendent, Judge Good, in common with every patriotic man in the land, felt the degredation to which his fellow citizens were reduced. At the earliest opportunity, which was not until 1871, he took the stump and hurled defiance at the oppressions and oppressors then weighing upon the people, appealing to all who were allowed to, to register and vote.

With John Henry Brown he canvassed several counties in this behalf and the result of their joint labors, assisted by others of the same faith, was that the people carried the elections in 1872, secured a legislature in sympathy with the masses and broke the chains of despotism in so far that the next year the people elected a full quota of state officers and a legislature representative of their will. In those days, when Judge Good forsook self and hazarded all on the cast of a die, many gentlemen of ability remained quiescent at home—some advising abject submission to the ruling power, others a prudence amounting to moral cowardice, and yet others contended that all efforts at redemption would be fruitless.

The state redeemed, Judge Good remained quietly at the bar, until taken up by the people and elected mayor of Dallas in August, 1880.

He has been for many years an active Mason and Odd Fellow, attained to the highest degrees of each order, and is a zealous worker in them. He has a handsome home and large plat of ground in Dallas, and is surrounded by a devoted wife and children. He also has considerable other property elsewhere and has stock in several local enterprises, and altogether, considering the travail of the country and that he is yet but in middle life, he has much for which to be thankful, not the least of which is the esteem in which he is held by those who have known him longest and best.

JUDGE ASA HOXIE WILLIE.

GALVESTON.

ASA HOXEY WILLIE is a native of Washington, Wilkes county, Georgia, and was born October 11, 1829. His father was James Willie, of Vermont, who, until his marriage, was a merchant; but having acquired some property by his wife, became a farmer; a quiet, retiring man, who died when his son was but four years old. His mother, still living, is a daughter of Asa Hoxey, a Massachusetts Quaker, who emigrated from Sandwich, on Cape Cod. The genealogy of the mother is distinctly traceable back to A. D. 1660, and somewhat less distinctly back to A. D. 1000.

Asa H. Willie, left fatherless at the age of four, had not the advantages of a liberal education and a collegiate course, but through the industry and economy of his mother, obtained at the Washington Academy, (which school he attended until he was fifteen years of age,) such training as could be afforded by one of the best high schools of that day. When sixteen years of age he assisted a cousin in teaching school, and taught while a student to get money to move to Texas, which he did in February, 1846, being then only a little over sixteen. He located at Independence, Washington county, and made his home with his uncle, Asa Hoxey, pursuing the study of the law and the Spanish language. This uncle came to Texas in the winter of 1833-4 and was a member of what is called the consultation, which was really the provisional government of Texas. He was a very large landholder and slaveholder, and was noted for his benevolence and hospitality, but was not a man to seek position, and the nephew has ever had the same aversion to public life. Asa H. Willie was admitted to the bar by an act of the legislature in 1848. He settled and began practice in Brenham, Washington county, and there remained eight or nine years. In 1857 he removed to Austin and remained in the office of his brother, James Willie, at that time attorney-general of the state and commissioner for codifying the laws of Texas.

The following year Mr. Willie removed to Marshall, and entered into partnership with his brother-in-law, Colonel Alexander Pope, with whom he practiced from 1858 till 1866, a period of eight years. In the latter year he moved to Galveston and formed a partnership in the practice of law with the distinguished Judge J. F. Crosby, of Houston, a friend of his boyhood. In June, 1871, he effected a partnership with Judge Charles L. Cleveland, and that partnership has continued to the present time.

In August, 1852, while residing at Brenham, Mr. Willie was elected prosecuting attorney of the then third judicial district of Texas. He held the office six months by appointment and two years by election, but declined a re-election at the close of his term. In 1866 he was elected by the people of Texas a justice of the supreme court for a term of nine years. At the end of fifteen months service he was removed by military authority. General Griffin, commanding the department of Texas, removed all the civil officers of the state from governor down to justices of the peace, Judge Willie being one of the number. In 1872 he was elected to the forty-third congress from the state at large and served his full term. In congress he devoted his attention to the local interests of Texas, the improvement of Galveston harbor, frontier protection and other matters in which the Southwest was especially interested. He was a member of the committee on commerce. On the 17th of March, 1874, he delivered in the hall of the house of representatives one of the ablest pleas and most convincing arguments in behalf of appropriations for the improvement of Galveston harbor, made during that session of congress on commercial matters. He presented the recent growth and activity of Galveston and its importance as a port of exit and entry; the vast empire behind it laden with semi-tropical products for exportation; the small and inadequate appropriations for the improvement of a harbor that ranks eighth in the amount of its annual exportations the utter neglect with which Galveston had been treated up to 1867 the millions that had been lavished upon the New England, Middle and Western states; the condition of the harbor for many successive years and the manner in which the energies of commerce had been paralyzed from want of ship channels into the harbor; the cost of the needed improvements, and the immense benefits that would accrue to the state and country by the judicious expenditure of a comparatively small sum upon the passes into Galveston bay. His speech showed great research and careful attention to details, and was printed in pamphlet form and extensively circulated and read in the Southwest.

At the close of his congressional term Judge Willie consented to become city attorney for Galveston, and served in that capacity in 1875-6.

His military history may be embraced in a small compass, not because it was by any means valueless, but because it was comparatively uneventful. He enlisted in the Confederate army in 1861, and served through the war. He was on the staff of General John Gregg, occupying at different times the positions of commissary, aid-de-camp, etc. During the last eleven months of the war he was stationed by General Kirby Smith at San Antonio to supervise the exportation of cotton. In his active campaigns he took part in the battles of Port Hudson, Chickamauga, Missionary Ridge, the siege of Jackson and other engagements of less note.

Asa H. Willie and Bettie Johnson were married at Marshall, Texas, October 20, 1859. Her father was Lyttleton Johnson, a merchant of Bolivar, Tennessee,

who died when his daughter Bettie was an infant. Soon after his death she was taken to Brandon, Mississippi, where subsequently her mother married William C. Harper, by whom she was reared. He died in 1869. Judge Willie and wife have seven living children, three having died young.

Judge Willie has led an active life, which has been devoted almost exclusively to his profession, and has amassed considerable property. He owns a very desirable residence on the corner of Broadway and Fifteenth streets, Galveston. The house is of peculiarly southern architecture, roomy and comfortable without being showy. He is a shareholder in the Texas Banking and Insurance Company and a stockholder in other moneyed corporations. His principal estate, the proceeds of his first fee as an attorney, (the case having lasted twenty-five years,) is in Williamson county, and consists of 4,000 acres of land, as valuable as any in the state. He also owns wild lands in Fannin, San Jacinto, Liberty, Brazoria and other counties, amounting to 6,000 or 7,000 acres.

Judge Willie has always been a Democrat and voted for secession. He has, however, in good faith accepted the results of the war and the reconstruction that has followed it. He is not connected with any religious society, but he was reared in the faith of the Methodist Episcopal church, his mother being a member of that denomination. The wife of Judge Willie is an Episcopalian. He became an Odd Fellow in 1854.

When General Lamar was appointed by President Buchanan to be minister resident in the Argentine Republic, he selected Judge Willie to be his secretary of legation, who accepted the position and started with him. But when the destination of General Lamar was changed to Nicaragua, Judge Willie declined going.

Some of the relatives of Judge Willie have been distinguished in the forum, at the bar and in the republic of letters. Colonel Alexander Pope, his partner and brother-in-law, was for a long time a member of the Georgia state senate; was a member of the convention that passed the ordinance of secession in Texas in 1861, and was known as a brilliant orator. He died in July, 1872.

His cousin, Miss Fanny Andrews, daughter of Garnett Andrews, is an authoress, writing over the *nom de plume* of Elzey Hay. She wrote "*A Mere Adventure*," a novel; also one entitled "*A Family Secret*," and others. Her home is in Washington, Wilkes county, Georgia.

His maternal uncle, Dr. Thomas Hoxey, of Columbus, Georgia, was an eminent physician and made a large fortune. His son, John Bulow Hoxey, was on General Rusk's staff and took part in the battle of San Jacinto. He afterwards practiced medicine in Galveston.

His cousin Annulett Ball, married Garnett Andrews, who was for twenty years judge of the superior court of Georgia, and the nominee of the American party for governor of that state in 1855, but was defeated by a small majority by Herschel V. Johnson.

One of her sons, Garnett Andrews, is a prominent lawyer in Mississippi. Another cousin, Dr. D. S. Ball, was a leading physician in New Orleans.

His brother, James Willie, his partner at Brenham, was attorney-general of Texas from 1856 to 1858; was the author of the criminal code and the code of criminal procedure; a member of the first two legislatures of the state from Washington county; brought Judge Willie to Texas, and was probably the best natural lawyer of his day. He died March 5, 1863.

His only living brother, William Thomas Willie, is a farmer living at Independence; has quite a genius for mechanics, and has invented and patented several useful devices.

His sister married Colonel Alexander Pope, and died in September, 1864, aged thirty-nine. She left nine children. One of her sons, John H. Pope, is an eminent physician and surgeon; was president of the State Medical Association, and inspector of the National Board of Health, and author of several noted essays in medical journals. Another son, William H. Pope, was county attorney, residing at Marshall, and like his younger brother, Alexander, has made quite a reputation as an orator. Three of her sons, James W., John H. and William H., were in the Confederate army, John H. having been severely wounded.

Judge Willie is an able and popular lawyer. He is a man of compact build, five feet ten inches high, weighing one hundred and seventy pounds, and capable of undergoing a great deal of labor. He is not yet an old man, and Texas has reason to expect of him further labors in her behalf. He is universally respected, and though not an office seeker, his eminent abilities may be still further drafted on for services to his adopted state.

[handwritten annotation spanning the column:] ye Willie was elected to the office of Chief Justice of ye Court of Texas in Nov 1882 which office he now — His opinions as Ch Justice will be found in 58 Texas Rep & onwards.

COLONEL DeWITT CLINTON STONE.

GALVESTON.

THE warp and woof of historical narrative must be made of facts, and when men are like Colonel DeWitt Clinton Stone, whose career has been marked alone with deeds of honor, no retiring dislike for the world's plaudits should be allowed to shade or pale the brilliancy of the shining virtues of his character. When one's virtues veil themselves in a sensitive shrinking from the glare of public praise, it is difficult indeed to weave a robe of honor with which to drape their proudly modest form; especially when the biographer is compelled, in some degree, to depend upon the man himself for much of his personal history. The influence of a good man will be ever expanding with the lapse of time, and his deeds of kindness, his acts of love, will live to commemorate his name, to perpetuate his memory. Men are only great from the standpoint of our observation, but there can be no power greater than the influence of a noble life, nothing more lasting than " its foot-prints left on the sands of time."

DeWitt Clinton Stone was born at Hilliardston, in Nash county, North Carolina, on the 7th of October, 1825. Of his ancestors but little is known, save the fact that his grandfathers on both sides were planters, and were also Revolutionary soldiers. His father, Thomas Green Stone, a planter, finely educated, of great moral worth and character, served the county in many important positions, representing it in the state senate; was afterwards elected clerk of the senate, which position he held until his death, a period of seventeen consecutive years. He was a man of unostentatious character, but of much intelligence. He died at the early age of forty-six years, lamented by all who knew him. The resolutions of the state legislature on the event of his death bear evidence of the high esteem in which he was held by the body which he had served so long. His mother, Francis Yancey Hawkins, died at an early age, leaving only two children, a son and a daughter. The last mentioned married Rev. T. M. Jones, at present the president of Greensboro Female College, and died many years since, leaving the subject of this sketch the only immediate representative of the family.

Colonel Stone had all the advantages of a primary school, and was sent to the University of North Carolina, at Chapel Hill, where he graduated in 1846. From here he went to the law school of the late Chief Justice Pearson to prepare himself for the bar. He first entered upon the practice of law in Franklin county, and was elected prosecuting attorney for the state and served one term successfully, and soon after his re-election was married to Mary M. Yarbrough, second daughter of Richard Femur Yarbrough, a prominent and wealthy merchant of Louisburg. Shortly after his marriage, finding mercantile pursuits more congenial to his tastes than the law, he resigned his position as prosecuting attorney and entered into this business. Notwithstanding this he was elected county judge by the people, and made one of the trustees of the university by the state legislature.

In 1860 the subject of our sketch moved to Galveston and commenced the commission business, but the war between the states coming on the following year, and business prospects being destroyed, he entered into the service of the Confederate States, and was active in facilitating the introduction of supplies for the government. Though not in the field, he was an ardent friend of the Confederacy, and sank his all with the result.

Upon the termination of the war he returned to Galveston and resumed business, though broken down in fortune. He was elected three years in succession

president of the Cotton Exchange, and while holding this position was chosen by the people mayor of the city, with such a majority over his opponents, R. L. Fulton, then mayor, and Charles Leonard, ex-mayor of the city, as no man had ever received. In politics he has always been an unswerving Democrat, but has held no political office save that of mayor of the city.

He was married, 1850, to Mary Mildred Yarbrough, whose father was a man of marked character and business capacity, having amassed a fortune in those days. She was educated at St. Mary's Hall, Raleigh, North Carolina, under the late Dr. Smedes; was distinguished for her gentleness of manners, close application, ready genius, and high standing in her classes; now a woman of rare grace and loveliness, who has twined about his life the sweetest of womanly affection, sharing alike his many public honors and his few private sorrows. Lovely and amiable, Mrs. Stone has indeed been to her husband even as a lamp to his feet, the light of his heart and life. Wearing the bright crown of motherhood gracefully, her children have grown up about her a blessing to both herself and husband; and if three little graves have cast deep shadows across their threshold, the sunny lives of their remaining three children, two sons and one daughter, have at least brightened the gloom and lifted the curtains of grief from the consecrated chamber in their hearts. Mrs. Stone has ever been to her husband the brightest star of his home and the dearest jewel of his heart.

> The best and noblest part of man's life here,
> Is that wherein he loves and honors woman.
> 'Tis then his soul is lifted to a higher sphere;
> In all things else, his nature is but human.

Colonel Stone is a rare instance of an open, generous, impulsive and highly vitalized nature, devoted from youth to middle age to mercantile pursuits, with occasional episodes of politics, without a trace of demoralization. He has the warmth of youth without its fever, the mellowness of age without its frosts. He still adheres to the busy man of offices, and no appeal for personal or pecuniary aid is ever made to him in vain. He has been conspicuous from his youth up for an uncommonly fine person, courtly bearing, flowing, cordial manners, ready conversational gifts, the most delicate sense of honor, and withal, the most unaffected modesty. Without seeking popular favor, he has always possessed it in an uncommon degree. Whilst habitually shunning, with the instincts of a fine nature, the public gaze, he has never failed to have accorded to him a prominent and influential position among his fellow men. Fitted for almost any public trust, he has wisely, and not less usefully, chosen to illustrate in his own person the virtues and graces which combine to form the character of a gentleman, pure and simple.

The elder son, Heber Stone, was sent to the University of the South at fifteen years of age, remained there one year, was then entered at the University of Virginia, where he remained until the completion of his college course; returned home and read law in the office of General Wane, a distinguished lawyer of Galveston, was admitted to the bar at twenty years of age, delivered an address before the Historical Society, of much merit for one so young. Soon after obtaining license to practice law, he settled himself in Brownwood, Texas, and was soon after elected county attorney, which office he resigned. He was married on the fourth of June, 1879, to Louise, only daughter of the late L. D. Giddings, a distinguished lawyer and banker, of Brenham, Texas, and is now a resident of that city and is engaged in the banking business, being a member of the firm of Giddings & Giddings. He has a fine personal presence, a cultivated manner, and is distinguished for great moral worth. His extreme devotion and love for his mother has been one of the marked characteristics of his life.

Clinton Stone, the second son, has been employed in the office of his father in the cotton business, is apt and sprightly, and bids fair to make a fine business man. He is too young to have developed any decided character.

Mary is the only daughter, is now (1880) at school in St. Mary's, in Raleigh, North Carolina. She is a lovely child, just budding into rosy girlhood. These children are the pride and pleasure of their parents. Father, mother, brothers and sister, constituting one of the happiest families the writer ever knew.

GENERAL JOHN R. JEFFERSON.

SEGUIN.

JOHN R. JEFFERSON was born May 11, 1804, in Cumberland county, Virginia. His grandfather, John Jefferson, was one of the two brothers who settled, and at one time owned half of Cumberland county; he was a cousin of President Thomas Jefferson, they being the sons respectively of Field and Thomas Jefferson, two brothers; was at one time sheriff of Cumberland; married a cousin of Lord Brougham; was immensely wealthy, three hundred negroes having been sold from his plantation at one time, leaving many still his property. His father, John Jefferson, was born in Cumberland county, a man of leisure and pleasure, who cared more to enjoy than to accumulate wealth. It is a singular fact that most of the issue of the Jefferson family have been females; the name is dying out, the subject of this sketch having one brother and six sisters, which is a fair sample of the proportion of males and females. John Jefferson, father of John R. Jefferson, married Miss Sarah Criddle, a native of Cumberland, born in 1785. Her father, John Criddle, was a farmer and a soldier of the Revolution. The Criddles were a family of plain people, never particularly distinguished, but good farmers and wealthy. John has been heard to say that there never was but one really great man in the Jefferson family—President Thomas Jefferson. Ann S. Jefferson, sister of John R., married Dr. John P. Ford, and her daughter, Della, is the wife of Dr. John Calender, superintendent of the Nashville Lunatic Asylum.

John Jefferson died when young John was but twelve years old, and his widow moved to Nashville, Tennessee, in 1818. Here John lived eleven years. In 1829 he went to New Orleans and engaged in staging. From 1832 to 1868, he was extensively engaged in stage contracts, some of which amounted to $100,000 per annum. He was twice a resident of New Orleans, the first time from 1829 to 1833. In the latter year he moved to Clinton, Hinds county, Mississippi, where he lived for twenty years. In 1853 he moved to Seguin, Texas, and has ever since made that his home.

For a period of twenty-five years he employed about one thousand head of horses in his various stage lines in the states of Missouri, Arkansas, Mississippi and Alabama. From 1854 to 1858 he had several lines of stages in Texas; but as the business required him to travel a great deal, he abandoned it and began the more agreeable and independent business of farming.

He is at present the owner, besides a few lots of an acre each in Seguin and considerable personal property, of a fine farm of two hundred and fifty acres adjoining the town, one hundred and seventy-five acres of which are in cultivation. He values his land at thirty dollars per acre, and the fruitful soil and varied products of this farm make the valuation very low. His land will yield an average annual crop per acre of one thousand pounds of seed cotton, thirty bushels of corn, sixty of oats, sixteen of wheat, forty of rye, and sorghum enough to make five hundred gallons of syrup. Millet yields two tons per acre, or forty bushels of seed. From seven acres of ground he has threshed three hundred bushels of seed, and the straw after the threshing was worth as much as common hay, the millet seed selling readily at three dollars per bushel. Fruits are abundant. Peaches have failed but once in twenty years. Early apples, pears, plums, etc., yield well. The Guadalupe river falls are on this land, and furnish fine water power. Mesquite timber, rich in tannin, is abundant, while hackberry, mulberry, box-alder, black walnut, sycamore, pecan and white oak with its festoons of moss are the principal forest growths. The country is unusually healthy, and endemic malarial diseases are almost unknown. From June to September the mercury ranges from eighty to one hundred degrees Fahrenheit during the day, while cool and refreshing sea or gulf breezes cool and make pleasant the nights. The population of his section is of a peaceful and law abiding class, both white and colored. Seguin is growing steadily, and the country is filling up with

first class citizens. Religious and political toleration is the rule.

During his residence in Mississippi he was a brigadier-general of militia from 1842 to 1846. He was married in Hinds county, Mississippi, June 4, 1841, to Miss Eliza A. Coorpender, daughter of Dr. Lewis Coorpender, a native of the "Old North State." She was born in 1826 at Raleigh, North Carolina. Her mother was a Miss Fenner, daughter of Dr. Robert Fenner, of Jackson, Tennessee. Her uncle, Dr. Erasmus Fenner, was the founder of the first medical journal established in New Orleans. She has five uncles who are physicians, and her people on both sides are prosperous in business and professional life.

General Jefferson and his wife had ten children, five of whom are living. Eugenia, born in Hinds county, Mississippi, in 1849; educated at Athens, Alabama, and Seguin, Texas; married first to Dudley Jeffreys, and after his death to Frank Saunders, of Seguin. John R., born in Clinton, Mississippi, in 1851; educated in Texas; entered the army at an early age; married Miss J. P. Miller, and has five children; is a prosperous farmer, rearing fine cattle being a specialty. His five children are John R., Robert M., Elizabeth, Anna, and Mary Lou. Fenner, born in Clinton, Mississippi, in 1852; educated at Seguin, now living with his father. Betty Howard, born in Seguin in 1858, and educated there; still under the paternal roof. Mary Lou, born in Seguin in 1860; married W. H. Burges, the well known criminal lawyer, orator and politician of Seguin. The following children of General Jefferson are dead: Mattie, born in Mississippi in 1843, educated in Texas, Mississippi and New Orleans; in 1865, was married to Haywood Brahan, son of R. W. Brahan, formerly of Huntsville, Alabama; died August, 1877, leaving five children, Annie, Robert, Haywood, Eugenia and Erskine, the latter of whom lived but one year. The others died in infancy.

General Jefferson is a Master Mason and a member of the Episcopal church, the church of his ancestors. He is a life-long Democrat, as all his family are or have been.

He has several times been the possessor of a large fortune. By the failure of the banks in 1839 he lost $300,000, but his credit was not impaired nor was his estate exhausted. He has been at all times the advocate of Colonel Benton's financial policy, opposed to banks and in favor of "hard money." He made several fortunes by staging, and as a contractor he always stood high, as his accounts with the postoffice department show.

He has ever been convivial, but though as strongly tempted as most men, was never intoxicated in his life. His energy was remarkable. He acted upon the principle that he could endure and do whatever any other man could. He was ever self-reliant, and while he sometimes counseled with others, he always relied on his own judgment. He had an intuitive knowledge of men, and read them with great facility. Hence his agents rarely disappointed him. He is a lover of horses and other stock, of which he is confessedly an excellent judge. His farming operations have been successful. Though nearly seventy-seven years of age and compelled to walk with crutches, his mind is yet vigorous and active. He is very companionable in society, communicative without volubility, and pleasing without gayety. He is descending the shadowy slope gracefully, with heart kindly disposed toward all, and enjoying the fruits of an active and useful life.

In height he is six feet and weighs one hundred and sixty pounds. His eyes are blue, his hair thin and silvery and his beard white as snow. General Jefferson has been worth a quarter of a million dollars, but lost most of his immense fortune. No man in Mississippi was better known than he.

During the Rebellion he was Confederate States marshal for the western district of Texas, and gave general satisfaction. In 1865 he broke his hip joint, and since then has been compelled to use crutches. He and his family have the respect of Seguin society, of which they form a conspicuous and important part.

REV. GEORGE WAVERLEY BRIGGS.

GALVESTON.

GEORGE WAVERLEY BRIGGS was born in Greensboro, Hale county, Alabama, December 14, 1851. His father, Rev. A. J. Briggs, is also a native of Greensboro; has been a devoted minister of the Alabama Conference of the Methodist Episcopal Church South many years; has been stationed at some of the most important cities of the state; was a presiding elder, and is still a member, of the Alabama Conference. His mother is a daughter of Samuel C. Brewer, now of Mississippi, and was born in Danville, Virginia, in 1832. She was thoroughly educated, and took special pains to superintend the education of her children. Mr. Briggs has one brother in the ministry, Rev. Ritchie J. Briggs, born November 21, 1853, educated at Greensboro, became a minister in 1873, is now a member of the Alabama Conference, stationed at Camden, is the orator, poet, pride and pet of the family.

George W. Briggs had superior educational advantages. He was reared a student, and did little or no manual labor. Before he was sixteen he entered the Southern University at Greensboro, and afterwards spent a year in the High School at Eufaula. Later he was a student in East Alabama College. His father moved to Summerfield, Alabama, and and young Briggs, having resolved to study law, began the study of that science in the office of Judge Woods, in Selma. His earliest predilections, however, were for the ministry, and a conflict arose in his mind between what he felt was a duty and his disposition to engage in a lucrative profession. This conflict resulted in a triumph of duty, and he laid aside his law books and entered the Southern University in 1872. The following year he graduated as bachelor of philosophy under Chancellor A. S. Andrews, D. D. This closed his collegiate course.

In his twenty-second year he was licensed to preach, and was received into the Alabama Conference in 1873. Two years later he was ordained a deacon at Greenville by Bishop Marvin, and an elder in 1877 by Bishop Keener, at Montgomery, being then in his twenty-sixth year. He was immediately transferred to the Texas Conference. In 1878, by Bishop Wightman's request and appointment, he took charge of St. James church, in Galveston, of which he had charge two years. In 1880, by Bishop McTyiere, he was transferred to St. John's church in the same city, of which he is is still (1881) the pastor. The church edifice, located on the corner of Broadway and Bath avenue, is a two-story brick, built in gothic style, and having beside the main audience room, (which has a seating capacity of 1,000, and a $5,000 organ,) a Bible class room, an infant class room, a Sunday school room and a pastor's room. The latter contains portraits of former pastors of the church, the most noted of whom were Rev. J. E. Walker, D. D., now pastor of the Carondelet Street church, New Orleans; Rev. General L. M. Lewis, who has recently accepted the presidency of Waxahachie College, and Rev. Wm. Shappard, D. D., now pastor of the First Methodist church at Austin. The building is the most complete and elegant Methodist Episcopal church in the West, south of St. Louis. The membership numbers three hundred and fifty, and probably represents as much wealth as any Methodist congregation in the Gulf states.

Mr. Briggs has won his position by devotion to his work. He has had the highest love for his profession, and has labored with the greatest enthusiasm. Although still young he has studied natures closely, and his illustrations are drawn from the every-day occurrences and common affairs of life. His sermons are practical, and are prepared evidently with labor and and care. He speaks without manuscript, or even notes, but is never diverted from the thread of his discourse. If there is an apparent digression it is for a purpose and forms part of the rounded and perfect whole. All Christian denominations listen with pleasure to his sermons, and the young of both sexes, with whom he is immensely popular, flock to his church. Without being sensational, he is an earnest preacher; but he does not belong to the class denominated revivalists. His pictures of home touch the hearts of the strangers, who form so large a part of the population of Galveston and of his audiences. His daily walk is in keeping with his high calling, and his character as a minister and a man is blameless. His diction is pure, well selected and adapted to the subject under examination. He has grand thoughts which he clothes in such language as the illiterate may grasp and understand. His descriptive powers are unsurpassed. His figures are apt, his arguments imposing, and his persuasive eloquence such as rarely fails to reach his auditors.

Mr. Briggs has already achieved much, and he has before him a grand field for the exercise of his abilities. He is a good student, his mind being of that inquisitive character not readily satisfied with surface gleanings. The truth is sought, and the ultimate truth whenever and wherever it can be found. Few young men have so suddenly risen to eminence, and fewer still have more thoroughly deserved distinction.

COLONEL WILLIAM W. FONTAINE, A. M.

AUSTIN.

WILLIAM WINSTON FONTAINE was born at Montville, King William county, Virginia, November 27, 1834. His father, William Spotswood Fontaine, was born in Hanover county, Virginia, November 7, 1810; received a full classical education; was married July 5, 1832; settled in King William county; in early life represented that county in the state legislature for several sessions; was commissioned colonel of the county regiment; about 1852 withdrew from political life, and was ordained a minister of the Baptist denomination, and is living at present, in full mental and physical strength, at Reidsville, North Carolina. He is of Huguenot extraction, being eighth in descent from a French nobleman and officer in the household of Francis I, John De la Fontaine, martyred in 1563; ancestor of all the Fontaines and Maurys in Virginia.

Rev. William Spotswood Fontaine's father, William Winston Fontaine, was the son of John Fontaine, and his wife, Martha, eldest daughter of Patrick Henry, the orator and governor of Virginia. Rev. William Spotswood Fontaine, through his mother, Martha, daughter of Nathaniel West Dandridge, jr., is the great-great-grandson of Major-General Alexander Spotswood, colonial governor of Virginia, the eleventh in descent from Sir Robert de Spottiswoode, born about 1249, of the barony of Spottiswoode, county of Berwick, Scotland. Governor Spotswood was thirteenth in descent from King Robert the Bruce, through his great-granddaughter, the Princess Catherine Stuart, fifth daughter of King Robert II and his first wife, Lady Elizabeth More. The Princess Catherine Stuart married David Lindsay, first Earl of Crawford. Rachel Lindsay, (daughter of Dr. David Lindsay, Bishop of Ross in 1600,) the seventh in descent from the Princess Catherine, married Archbishop John Spotswood, Lord High Chancellor of Scotland. Their son, Sir Robert Spotswood, Secretary of Scotland during the reign of Charles I, was executed January 17, 1646, on account of his adherance to the royal cause. Sir Robert's third son, Dr. Robert Spotswood, was the father of General Alexander Spotswood, governor of Virginia.

Nathaniel West Dandridge, jr., mentioned above, was the son of Colonel Nathaniel West Dandridge,

sr., who married Dorathea, youngest daughter of Governor Spotswood. (General Robert E. Lee was the great-grandson of Governor Spotswood's eldest daughter, Mrs. Ann Catherine Moore). Colonel Nathaniel West Dandridge, sr., was the son of Captain William Dandridge, H. B. M. navy, and Unity, daughter of Nathaniel West, son of Colonel John West, governor of Virginia, in 1635. Colonel Nathaniel West Dandridge, sr., was full brother to Mary, wife of Philip Aylett, and mother of Colonel William Aylett, commissary general. The mother of Colonel Fontaine was Miss Sarah Shelton Aylett, the daughter of Colonel Philip Aylett, of Montville, and his wife, Elizabeth Henry, third daughter of Patrick Henry. Patrick Henry was great-nephew, and Lord Brougham was grandson of William Robertson, the great historian. General Joseph E Johnston is great-nephew of Patrick Henry. She was born at Montville, June 24, 1811, and died in Reidsville, North Carolina, March 5, 1876. She was a woman of great suavity of manner, and remarkable for her intellectual power and personal beauty. Colonel Philip Aylett was the son of William Aylett, colonel and commissary-general of the southern department during the Revolution, and his wife, Mary, daughter of Colonel James Macon, and his wife, Elizabeth Moore, daughter of Colonel Augustine Moore, of Chelsea, King William county, Virginia.

R. A. Brock, the antiquary, in the Richmond Standard, says:

Among the older families of those long seated in Virginia, none are more highly esteemed than that of Aylett, which indeed may claim connection by intermarriage with quite all those of prominence in the state. But a glance at its lineal deduction will exhibit lustrous names which have adorned every period of her annals—pioneer, statesman, soldier, orator and scholar—all are represented.

The record of descent of this family, condensed from Burke's account, is as follows:

The Aylett or Ayloffe family is of Saxon extraction, being descended from one Alulphus, a Saxon. From this Alulphus descended Ayliff, a person of great note in the time of Edward the Confessor. About the reign of Henry VI, we find a descendant of this Ayliff, a certain John Ayloff, seated in Essex county, holding large possessions. The sixth in descent from this John Ayloff was Sir Benjamin Ayloffe or Aylett, the name

ment and so remained two years. He next became
vice president and professor in the Female College of
Mansfield, Louisiana, serving also a year as pastor of
the church.

At Mansfield, in 1858, Mrs. Pitts died, leaving five
children. In the year 1857 he first met his present
wife, Miss Sallie J. McNeeley, a teacher in the Female
College at Mansfield. They were subsequently married at Auburn, Alabama. She was the daughter
of Richard and Sarah McNeeley, small farmers, near
Oak Bowery, Alabama, and was the eldest of a family of seven children. She had no opportunities for
education except in the small country schools, near
her home, until she had fully entered her teens.
Then accident threw the Reverend George Chatfield
in her way. Ill-health sent him into the country, and
he took charge of Sardis Academy, an institution
one-eighth of a mile distant from her father's. In this
school she exhibited such marked mental ability that
Mr. Chatfield determined that she should be educated for a teacher, if her parents approved. Neither
they nor herself had ever dreamed that in the simple, unaffected, country girl there were powers capable of the highest culture; and when her father was
convinced of the fact, he left no stone unturned in the
accomplishment of the object. When first the fires of
thought were kindled in her mind, there arose an
almost insatiable thirst for knowledge. She loved it
for itself, and after she entered college, she had no
thought but for her books. Her march was rapid.
Her studies were directed with the view of making her
a teacher. In 1855 she graduated from Oak Bowery
College with the highest honors. She immediately
became a teacher in that institution; but in a few
months found a more lucrative position in LaFayette
College, where she remained a year; then taught a
private school one year, when she was offered and
accepted a good situation in the Female College at
Homer, Louisiana, where one of her former teachers
was principal. After one year she accepted a position
in Mansfield College, of which Dr. Pitts was a professor. She remained a year and then returned to Alabama, to take position in the institution in which she
had graduated, but which had been removed to Tus-

kegee and re-established as Tuskegee College. Dr.
Pitts soon followed and married her. Beside her at
the altar stood her old preceptor, Professor Chatfield,
and her maternal uncle, Rev. T. J. Williamson. Dr.
Pitts had just become president of the college at
Auburn, and she at once entered upon duty as his
assistant in the mathematical department, and has
ever since been his co-worker. Two years later
Dr. Pitts became president of the academy at Pratt-
ville, Alabama, and, in 1862, of the Opelika Female
College, where Mrs. Pitts first developed her superior
talents as a music teacher, which has ever since been
of her forte. In 1871 Wesleyan Female College,
Macon, Georgia, conferred upon her the first hon-
orary degree, an honor yet bestowed upon but five
other ladies. This college is the first in the world
clothed with authority by law to confer degrees upon
ladies.

In August, 1872, Dr. Pitts was chosen president
of Chappell Hill Female College, the oldest in the
state of Texas. He remained in that position seven
years, and was then elected to the same trust in the
North Texas Female College at Sherman.

Mrs. Pitts, though of delicate frame, continues an
indefatigable helpmate to her husband in the college,
has nurtured, beside her own, her husband's first set
of children, one of his sisters and two of her own,
besides presiding over her own domestic affairs—
verily, a true and noble woman.

By his first marriage Dr. Pitts had five children:
Anna N., married and died soon after; Julia H. C.,
Mary E., and Susan A., reside with their husbands,
in Washington county, Texas. Epaminondas died an
infant soon after his mother.

By the second marriage there have been born four
children: Walter A., a promising young man; the
next died at birth; Edgar M. died in infancy; Jonne-
maie is a bright little school girl.

Dr. Pitts is a Democrat, has been thirty-three years
a Mason, but does not meddle in politics, preferring
to devote his whole time to the calling to which he
has consecrated so many years of his life—the education of the young. Such men are rare and deserve
the esteem of the wise and the good.

COLONEL JAMES BOWIE.

MARTYR OF THE ALAMO.

THERE has never appeared anything approach-
ing a full and correct memoir of this remarkable
man. Fugitive anecdotes and incidents, often apoc-
ryphal, have been published from time to time, chiefly
devoted to the rougher side of his character, till the
popular mind has long regarded him as a combination
of gambler, soldier, ruffian and desperado. The
writer laments that he cannot supply the void. In
vain, through friends in New Orleans, he has sought
to recover a memoir, once in his possession, written

in modest simplicity, by his brother, John J. Bowie,
of Mississippi, twenty-nine years ago, and the only
authoritative statement known to him, ever given of
the parents, birthplace and the brothers and sisters of
Bowie. He deplores this failure and must rely, as
others have done, on the somewhat accidental sources
of information. It may be said, however, that his
father was a man of high moral character and inflexible integrity, while his mother was a devotedly pious
woman—both natives of Prince George's county,

Maryland, where their children were born. The sons were David, James, Resin P., John J. and Stephen, all large and muscular men. The Bowie family of Maryland has long been distinguished for wealth, education and high social position, as well as in politics and jurisprudence. The parents of James Bowie, however, sometime between 1802 and 1810, settled on the Mississippi, in Louisiana, not far from Natchez, Mississippi. Their sons were highstrung men, of fine address, endued with the spirit of enterprise and adventure; but James and Resin P. were the only ones who figured in Texas.

James Bowie, prior to coming to Texas was a general trader in the "lower country," interested in planting, but dealing in horses, mules and to some extent in slaves. The oft-repeated story that he bought wild negroes from Lafitte and sold them to planters, is regarded as a myth, as dates do not give credence to it. Such an occurrence may possibly have happened in some isolated instance, but, as a business, it is contradicted by his age and the final departure of Lafitte from the Gulf coast. That he was even a professional gambler is untrue; but it is true that he was an adept in the games of chance then common in the Valley of the Mississippi, from Galena to New Orleans, and, on rare occasions, he was lucky in winnings—oftener, however, to recover the losses of an unfortunate friend than to win for himself. Of this numerous instances were wont to be narrated by his old friends.

He was ever passionately fond of hunting and wild adventure—his mind dwelling much on the discovery of gold and silver mines—in which he spent much time in Texas. It was while wounded, on one occasion, that he modeled in wood, with his pocket-knife, and on recovering, had a blacksmith to fabricate what has since been so universally known as the "Bowie-knife." He had no thought in its creation but that of an improved knife for sticking and skinning game, and its still universal use for such purposes is a tribute to his ingenuity.

It is commonly said that he first came to Texas in 1828; but this is clearly a mistake. He probably made a tour of the country in 1824 and certainly did in 1826. Perhaps not till 1828 was his business so arranged in Louisiana as to warrant his constant residence in Texas.

He married a daughter of Lieutenant-Governor Veremendi, of an old Castilian family—a pure and charming woman, to whom he was devotedly attached and was equally loved in return. She bore him two or three children; but herself, father and children fell victims to the cholera in 1832 or 1834, and Bowie never ceased to mourn for them. To some extent he became a changed man by this great calamity.

Of the celebrated sand-bar fight in front of Natchez, in 1828, in which he, his brother Resin P. and other friends were on one side, and an equal number on the other, it can only be said that it was a desperate and bloody affair, with loss of life and blood on each side. It was a wholesale duel, arranged by

agreement and the result of a feud among fearless, not to say reckless, men. It is said that Bowie while down and unable to rise from a wound, grappled his erect antagonist and killed him with his knife. The survivors, however, separated, never more to renew the contest, and Bowie to recover from his ugly wounds.

His first distinguished action in Texas, was in a fight, while en route from San Antonio to the old San Saba silver mines, which occurred six miles before reaching the mine on the 2d day of November, 1831. Bowie's party consisted of himself as chief, his brother, Rezin P. Bowie, David Buchanan, Robert Armstrong, Jesse Wallace, Matthew Doyle, Cephas Hamm, James Coriell (Coryell?) Thomas McCaslin and two servant boys, Charles and Gonzales. They had been advised by two friendly Comanches and a Mexican that they were followed by one hundred and twenty-four hostile Wacos and Tahuacanos and forty Caddos, who were determined to have their scalps. They chose as a night camp a cluster of thirty or forty liveoaks, with much underbrush. To the north was a thicket of oak bushes and near by a stream of water. They prepared for defence by clearing out the interior of the thicket into which their horses were placed. The Indians appeared at sunrise next morning and the battle began—one hundred and sixty-four Indians against nine men and two boys. With varying fortune the contest continued till sunset, when the Indians drew off never more to renew the attack, but to howl their lamentations all night. The Indians, as subsequently learned, lost eighty-two in killed and wounded. Bowie lost one man killed and three wounded. He remained in his covert eight days and was then twelve days in conveying his wounded back to San Antonio. In Yoakum's History and the Texas Scrap-Book will be found a full and graphic account of this most remarkable and heroic action.

The battle of Nacogdoches was fought August 2, 1832, and Colonel Piedras retreated west during the night of that day, but surrendered to an advance guard of only nineteen men and boys, on the morning of the 4th at the Angelina. Bowie arrived on the afternoon of the same day, the 4th of August. Piedras was escorted back to Nacogdoches and soon paroled. Bowie took charge of the six hundred Mexican soldiers and escorted them to the Rio Grande. On the old military road traveled there was not a house from Nacogdoches to San Antonio—unless a cabin on the Brazos and one at Bastrop, on the Colorado—nor a human habitation from San Antonio to the Rio Grande, in all about five hundred miles.

Burning for revenge on the Indians who had fought him on the San Saba, he took command of a company in the fall of 1832 to invade their country and made an extensive tour up the country from San Antonio and thence across to their chief resorts on the Brazos. But the savages learned of the movement and that Bowie, the "Fighting Devil" of their imagination, was at the head of it, and precipitately fled further into the wilderness. In a trip of six or seven hundred miles he never saw a single Indian. He returned greatly disappointed, but still resolved, at a more opportune season, to chastise them for their perfidy. The opportunity, however, never came.

When the revolution broke out, in 1835, Bowie joined the army at Gonzales, under General Stephen F. Austin, and moved with it upon San Antonio. From the camp on the Salado, Austin dispatched Bowie and Fannin, with ninety-two men, to reconnoitre and select a camp ground near the city. They encamped in a horse-shoe bend of the river immediately in front of the abandoned Mission of Concepcion, about two miles below the town, and passed the night, but just at dawn next morning, were furiously attacked by four hundred Mexicans, with a battery of small guns. The action was short and decisive. The Texians, protected by the river bank, dealt death to them so rapidly that they precipitately fled to the shelter of the city, leaving many dead, while our loss was but one man, Richard Andrews, killed. This was the 28th of October. On the 26th of November Bowie again displayed his prowess in the Grass Fight, near San Antonio on the west, when the enemy were driven headlong into the town.

At this time the provisional government was in its swaddling clothes in San Felipe. Bowie had no regular command. He was eager for active and honorable service and offered himself to the new tribunal; but the legislative council, charged with so many and grave responsibilities, failed to respond immediately to his applications for authority to raise and command a force. At least the delay was such as to cause Bowie to repair in person to the seat of government. His impetuosity could not brook delay, and after waiting some days, he suddenly appeared at the bar of the council and essayed to address the president of the body, "Order! order!" rang through the hall, while Bowie stood erect, hat in hand, the personification of splendid manhood and fierce determination. The air was full of revolution—Bowie, the idol of a majority of the people. A crisis was at hand. The presiding officer was Lieutenant-Governor James W. Robinson, one of the most talented, suave, bland and sagacious men in Texas. Quick as lightning he grasped the situation, and substantially said:

"Gentlemen of the council, while it is not strictly parliamentary, yet you certainly will not object to hearing the views of one so long-tried, distinguished and courageous as Colonel Bowie, on the condition of the country."

Instantly a motion was made and carried inviting Colonel Bowie to address the council.

This scene was afterwards described to me by Lieutenant-Governor Robinson, and I reproduce the remainder of the episode as nearly in his own words as a riveted memory can recall them.

Bowie was a splendid specimen of manhood—six feet and one inch high, straight as an arrow, of full but not surplus flesh, fair complexion, fine mouth, well-chiseled features and keen blue eyes—with grace and dignity in every movement. So far as known this was his first and last public speech. Stepping inside the railing, still hat in hand, with a graceful and dignified bow, he addressed himself to the president and council for nearly an hour in a vein of pathos, irony, invective and fiery eloquence that astounded and enraptured his oldest and most intimate friends. He reviewed the salient points of his life, hurled from him with indignation every floating allegation affecting his character as a man of peace and honor—admitted that he was an unlettered man of the Southwest, and his lot had been cast in a day and among a people rendered necessarily, from political and material causes, more or less independent of law; but brave, generous and infinitely scorning every species of meanness and duplicity; that he had honorably cast his lot with Texas for honorable and patriotic purposes; that he had even neglected his own affairs to serve the country in the hour of danger; had betrayed no man, deceived no man, wronged no man, and had never had a difficulty in the country unless to protect the weak from the strong and evil intentioned. That, yielding to the dictates of his heart, he had taken to his bosom as a wife a pure and lovely woman of a different race, the daughter of a distinguished "Coahuil-Texano," yet, as a thief in the night, death had invaded his little paradise and taken his father-in-law, his wife and his little jewels, given to him by the God his pious mother had taught him to reverence and to love as "Him that doeth all things well," and chasteneth those He loveth; and now, standing as a monument of Omnipotent mercy, alone of his blood in all Texas, all he asked of his country was the privilege, under its aegis, of serving it in a field where his name might be honorably associated with the brave and the true in rescuing this fair and lovely land from the grasp of a remorseless military despotism.

The effect was magical. Not an indecorous or undignified word fell from his lips—not an ungraceful movement or gesture—but there he stood, before the astonished council and spectators, the living exemplification of a natural orator.

He tarried not, but left, satisfied that in the more perfect organization of the government, he would receive generous consideration, and returned to San Antonio, soon to be immured in a sick room—a dark little cell-shaped room in the Alamo—and there, after a siege of thirteen days, to be perhaps the last of the hundred and eighty-two martyrs to yield up his life for his country; but not until, from that sick chamber, he had sent death through its door to a dozen or more of the assailants. Thus died Bowie, to be cremated by the order and in the presence of Santa Anna, along with his hundred and eighty-one comrades.

He was called "Colonel" by courtesy; but never actually held rank above captain of a company. One of the early acts of the republic was to perpetuate his name in a county in the northeast corner of the state, now traversed by three great railroads.

It was never my fortune to meet Colonel Bowie, but he was an intimate friend of my father and two of my uncles, one paternal, the other maternal, all men of peace, and neither of whom ever had a personal difficulty in Texas; and beyond this I enjoyed close associations in youth and early manhood with many good men who knew him long and well. Their universal testimony was that he was one of nature's noblemen, inflexible in honor, scorning double-dealing and trickery—a sincere and frank friend—kind and gentle in intercourse—liberal and generous—loving peace and holding in almost idolatry woman in her purity. He tolerated nowhere, among the rudest men, anything derogatory to the female sex, holding them as "but a little lower than the angels." In the presence of woman he was a model of dignity, deference and kindness, as if the better elements of his nature were led willing captive at the shrine of true womanhood. But, when aroused under a sense of intended wrong, and far more so for a friend than for himself, "he was fearful to look upon," and if, as happened at remote periods, under the influence of drink, he was a dangerous man to the wrong-doer. He was usually a man of few words, but exceedingly sociable and a good listener. Occasionally, especially when pleasantly situated with friends around the camp fire, his fine conversational powers came into play and he would talk long and rapidly of men and things, always to the gratification of listeners.

The preceding has all been written from information long in my possession; but recently it has been my good fortune to receive several notes of recollections of Colonel Bowie, from gentlemen who knew him well, and with pleasure they are submitted as a part of this memoir.

Captain William Y. Lacy, of Palestine, says:

Colonel Bowie was six feet one inch high, weighed two hundred pounds, was remarkably straight, square in form, walked erect, with firm step, had blue eyes, fair complexion, auburn hair, and was a man of commanding appearance. He was like Barnum's show, wherever he went everybody wanted to see him. From March, 1834, for eight months, I was with him, examining lands on the Trinity up to the Cross-timbers (now Tarrant county.) He was esteemed wealthy. He seemed to be a roving man—sometimes searching for mines, sometimes fighting Indians, sometimes speculating in lands, and always a gentleman from bottom to top. He was accommodating, kind and always had plenty of money. Bowie once described to me the sand-bar duel in front of Natchez. Bowie was shot down and one of the opposite party ran a swordcane through his breast. Bowie, reaching up, forked his antagonist down and killed him with his knife. He rarely referred to such things, but once showed me the sword wound. He seldom laughed, but always seemed firm, pleasant and cheerful. I always felt as if with a friend and a gentleman when with Bowie. He was neither austere, haughty nor easily insulted. He was a great hunter and a splendid shot—the best I ever saw—had an exceedingly open and frank countenance. He was not in the habit of using profane language, and never used an indecent or vulgar word during the eight months I passed with him in the wilderness.

Such is the testimony of Captain Lacy, a gentleman venerable in years and of the highest reputation for morality and integrity.

The venerable Captain Archibald Hotchkiss, of Palestine, now eighty-seven years of age and a graduate of the United States Military Academy at West Point, says:

I first met Bowie in Washington City in 1832. He was over six feet high, well proportioned, strong and muscular, with auburn hair and dark blue eyes. He was a splendid man in appearance, with intelligence and energy strongly marked on his face. In Washington he was finely but not gaudily dressed; but in Texas he usually dressed plainly. Again I saw him at the convention of April, 1833, in San Felipe, and, after its adjournment, traveled with him and a party of gentlemen to Brazoria. Among them were General Sam Houston, General John T. Mason, General Arnold, Samuel Sawyer, Captain Henry S. Brown, Thomas J. Chambers and Sterrit, who, I think was a brother-in-law of Bowie. Late in 1835 I traveled with him from San Antonio to San Felipe, whither he went on business with the provisional government. He was temporarily adjutant-general of the volunteer army before San Antonio and was dispatched to the Rio Grande to burn the grass on the route to prevent the advance of the Mexican cavalry and lancers, a duty which he promptly performed. Our companions en route to San Felipe were Dr. Richardson, William G. Logan and another, whose name I have forgotten. [Captain Hotchkiss confirms the previous statements in relation to the Natchez duel and continues:] Bowie was a very kind man, as his general conduct evinced. When he gave his friend his hand it was a pledge of fidelity never to be broken by him. It was generally said that he had been in several violent transactions, but not on his own account. But when he espoused the cause of a friend he would adhere to him to the bitter end, unless his confidence was betrayed. I do not know that he ever had a duel on his own personal account. He was a noble man, and I cherish his memory as a man of the strictest honor and a friend.

General J. E. Jefferson, of Seguin, Texas, says he knew Bowie in Natchez in 1829, traveled with him on steamboats and stopped with him at taverns; that he stood high as a citizen and a gentleman; that he was of incorruptible integrity, never violating plighted faith; that he was not a professional gambler, though he and almost every one in that section, in those days, would play poker and other games. He owned a fine plantation, called Sedalia, and negroes near Natchez, on the west side of the Mississippi. "Natchez under the hill," was then a sink of iniquity beyond realization at this day and gave very unjustly, a bad repute abroad to the whole surrounding country. It was the gateway of the Bowies from their home into Natchez and romance has connected their names with many affairs in it with which they had no connection whatever.

Mr. William McGinley, of Douglas, Kansas, says that he once traveled in a stage-coach in company with James Bowie, on the Cumberland road, across the Alleghanies. Besides them there were in the stage two men and a sick lady. The lady occupied the back seat, Bowie and McGinley the middle and the other two the front seat. [Henry Clay, of Kentucky, often told this story, as one of the other two passengers.] No one knew Bowie, who was silent and muffled up in a cloak. The unknown man on the front seat began smoking a cigar. The lady politely requested him to desist as it made her sick. He replied that he had paid his money to ride in the coach and would smoke as much as he pleased. Bowie sprang up, drew a Bowie-knife from behind his shoulders, and holding it before the smoker, said, "I give you one minute in which to throw that cigar away." It went overboard without awaiting the manner of its going. The knife was returned to its place and no further allusion made to the subject. Only at the

next stand was Bowie's identity ascertained. It is
well known that Mr. Clay often narrated this incident
as an eye-witness, and that he had a great admiration
for Bowie.

A distinguished gentleman, well known to the writer,
says that W. W. Bowie, a cousin of James, was one
of the most profound jurists of Baltimore, and that,
as a family, they all had talent, honor and fine culture. But a few years since one of the family was
several terms governor of Maryland, and that the
memory of James Bowie should be rescued from the
obloquy which, through ignorance and misconception,
has attached to his name in the minds of many persons. This gentleman is a minister of the Gospel
and a distinguished educator.

Captain William G. Hunt, an old resident of Columbus, Texas, and a man of unsullied character, who
came to Texas early in 1831, first met Colonel Bowie
and his wife at the house of his neighbor, Robinson,
on Christmas of that year. Bowie and wife were
en route on a visit to Louisiana, and Mr. Robinson
gave them a dinner to which the whole vicinity were
invited. Mrs. Bowie was a beautiful Castilian lady,
and won all hearts by her sweet manners. Bowie
seemed supremely happy with and devoted to her,
more like a kind and tender lover than the rough
backwoodsman he has since been represented to be.

On the 22d of February, 1881, there appeared in
the San Francisco *Chronicle* a communication in
regard to Colonel Bowie, signed L. P. H., which
bears upon its face such distinctive marks of personal knowledge and candor that I transcribe the sub-
joined extracts:

The writer says:

The account published in the *Chronicle* of February 23,
from the Philadelphia *Times*, of the "invention of the Bowie-
knife, and the duel in which it was first used," is incorrect in
so many particulars that I feel constrained to write out a true
history. I stood by the side of my father, among a number
of the citizens of the city of Natchez, and witnessed the fight
in question, and am willing to make oath that everything here
stated is strictly true.

The Bowie brothers were natives of the state of Maryland,
of a respectable family, into which Reverdy Johnson, the great
constitutional lawyer, married. They emigrated to Mississippi
in the year 1802 and engaged in the speculation of the rich
cotton and sugar lands of that section. The staple of cotton at
that period bearing almost a fabulous price gave great impetus
to land monopoly, and the Bowie brothers found themselves
confronted with another land speculating company, of which
the Judge Crain mentioned in the article of the Philadelphia
Times was the recognized head, both parties having a following of about seventy-five or one hundred men each, all men of
wealth and social position and all "on the fight." The Bowie
brothers were men of good physical stature, sinewy and of a
good, determined cast of countenance. Rezin was the most
considerate of the two, but James was brave to desperation.
It was frequently remarked of him that he was a "stranger to
the emotion of fear." They were both sportsmen—that is
they bet against the popular game of the day, faro, and played
"brag," the twin brother to poker. Judge Crain was chivalry
personified. He had emigrated from South Carolina to Louisiana. He was tall and strong and wholly fearless, or seem-
ingly so.

Now, as to the fight on the sandbar opposite the city of
Natchez. A challenge to fight a duel had passed between Dr.
Maddox, of the Crain party, and Samuel Wells, of the Bowie

party. According to the terms of the fight neither Judge
Crain nor James Bowie were to be present, because a deadly
feud existed between them. Bowie doubted that Judge Crain
would prove faithful to the agreement, and sent a courier to
spy his actions. The parties to the duel met, but friends from
the city of Natchez went over, and, through their influence,
restored amicable relations. To cement these relations the
parties sent across the river to Natchez for champagne, brandy
and Havana cigars. Circled around a spring which flowed
from the west bank of the river, all hostile feeling was swal-
lowed up by the generous liquid, and everything was tinged
with the rainbow hues of friendship, when Judge Crain put in
an appearance. He, too, joined in the conviviality, pleased
that no blood was to be shed. But there was another appearance to be made before another hour passed. While thus
pleasantly occupied a rustling was heard in the willow boughs
that overhung the steep bank that led down to the spring, and,
turning their faces, the manly form of James Bowie met
their eyes. His appearance meant fight, and at it they
went. Judge Crain was the first man who arose from his seat,
and with his pistol shot Bowie, the ball passing entirely
through his body, but failed to cut any cord which bound him
to life. Bowie fell and Judge Crain, with the spear in his
sword-cane, ran up and endeavored to stab him. Bowie skil-
fully parried the thrust of the spear, and, collecting his energies, reached up with his left hand and caught Judge Crain by
the cravat, which, according to the fashion of the day, was tied
securely around the neck. He drew him down close to his
body, with his right hand secured the spear and ran it through
his heart, Judge Crain dying upon the body of his prostrate
foe, who meantime fainted from the loss of blood. As soon as
Crain discharged the pistol the friendly feeling which previously
existed was dissolved quick as a snowflake falling on a heated
furnace, and the friends of the two parties separated and commenced firing on each other. Six were killed and fifteen
wounded. The writer hereof takes pleasure in stating that his
father was the first man who said: "Men, let us rush in
between them and stop the fighting."

James Bowie lay for months in his bed, in the city of
Natchez, before he recovered from his wound. He was a man
of much mechanical ingenuity, and while thus confined, whit-
tled from a piece of white pine the model of a hunting-knife,
which he sent to two brothers named Blackman, in the city
of Natchez, and told them to spare no expense in making a
duplicate of it in steel. This was the origin of the dreaded
Bowie-knife. It was made from a large saw-mill file, and its
temper afterward improved upon by an Arkansas blacksmith.
This is all that can be told about the origin of that death-deal-
ing implement.

Since James Bowie became prominent in his efforts to
advance the spread of republican institutions, it is proper to
speak of what he did. He seemed to have a natural disposition to protect the weak from the strong. One time he was
riding through the parish of Concordia, Louisiana, and saw a
man lashing his slave with his whip. He told the man to
desist, but he was met with curses. He dismounted from his
horse, wrested the whip from the master and laid it over his
shoulders. This led to a shooting-match, in which the slave-
owner was badly wounded. Bowie, after submitting himself
to the law, paid the doctor's bill, purchased the slave at double
his value and gave him his freedom.

At another time the son of William Lattimore, governor of
the Territory of Mississippi, a religious gentleman of literary
attainments, was sent by his father to the city of Natchez to
sell his year's crop of cotton. The "ropers-in" of faro games
made the acquaintance of the son, and induced him to patron-
ize the game of a certain gambler named Sturdevant, "under
the hill," at Natchez. The gambler soon had the proceeds of
the crop, in bank bills in his possession. Bowie, who was
standing by, a silent spectator, said to young Lattimore: "I
know you; you don't know me, but your father does; stand
here until I tell you to go. He then commenced betting at
Sturdevant's game, and discovering an unfair turn of the cards
told him sternly not to attempt the cheat again. He shortly

won back the amount young Lattimore had lost, gave the whole amount to him and told him never to gamble any more. This young Lattimore assented to, and faithfully did he keep his promise.

This led to the fight between Sturdevant and Bowie. The former hoping, it is presumed, to "bluff" Bowie, proposed to fight with knives, the left hand of each to be lashed together. Resin Bowie proposed to take his brother's place, as the latter had severely cut his hand in butchering a deer a short time previous. This proposition James Bowie indignantly rejected. The fight took place and at the first stroke Bowie disabled his antagonist, but magnanimously forebore to take his life.

In after years a Methodist preacher told the writer this: He said he was one of the first Methodist ministers sent to Texas by the Methodist Conference. He traveled on horseback, crossing the Mississippi river below Natchez; that the first day after crossing the Mississippi river he was overtaken by a horseman dressed in buckskin, armed with rifle, pistol and knife. They entered into conversation and he found him to be intelligent, pleasant and well acquainted with the geography of the country. Neither one inquired the name or business of the other. Both were aiming at the same destination, Texas. Finally they reached a new town filled with wild, desperate characters from other states. He posted a notice that he would preach at the court house the first evening of his arrival there. At the hour named he found the rude structure thronged to overflowing—with men only. He gave out a hymn, and all joined in singing, and sung it well, but when he announced his text and attempted to preach, one brayed in imitation of an ass, another hooted like an owl, etc. He disliked to be driven from his purpose and attempted again to preach, but was stopped by the same species of interruption. He stood silent and still, not knowing whether to vacate the pulpit or not. Finally his traveling companion, whom he did not know was in the house, arose in the midst and with stentorian voice said: "Men, this man has come here to preach to you. You need preaching to, and I'll be——if he shan't preach to you! The next man that disturbs him shall fight me. My name is Jim Bowie." The preacher said that after this announcement he never had a more attentive and respectful audience, so much influence had Bowie over that reckless and dangerous element.

I have thus sought, in the utmost good faith, with the limited means at hand, and very briefly, to present Colonel Bowie to those who live after him, as he was—noble, gifted in person and mind—fearless, generous and magnanimous—fervidly patriotic, overflowing with energy and enterprise—true in his affections,

frank in his professions, an affectionate son and brother and a devoted husband. His foibles—vices if the term be preferred—were incident to the times and places in which he lived. Few around him, in all his manhood, were exempt from them in greater or less degree. But while he stood aloft, maintaining an unchallenged integrity, with the respect and admiration of the best, thousands fell by the wayside. His name is forever linked with an immortal tragedy in the world's history, there to shine, as hero and patriot, till the genius of liberty shall retire into the caverns of darkness never to be pierced by the light of sun, moon or stars. Men may cease to venerate his memory—but WOMAN NEVER!

Of the Lieutenant-Governor Robinson mentioned in this sketch, may be added a few words: He came from Cincinnati to Nacogdoches in the winter of 1834-5, an able lawyer and fine orator. He served in the first Consultation of 1835, was made lieutenant-governor in the provisional government till March, 1836, and in the fall of that year was one of the first four district and ex officio supreme judges of the republic, resident at Gonzales, his district embracing all the country west of the Colorado. He resigned in January, 1840, and practiced law till 1849. He was taken prisoner with the court, bar and citizens, in San Antonio, September 11, 1842, imprisoned at Perote, released by special order of Santa Anna, and reached home in April, 1843. In 1849, with his wife and only child, William, a boy then about twelve, he went overland to San Diego, California, where he died a few years later. In Arizona they were held in captivity several days by Indians and robbed, but not otherwise injured. During the late war William came back to Texas and gallantly commanded a company in the Confederate army. Since then he has been sheriff and representative of San Diego county, and was living there when last heard from. Judge Robinson often expressed his great admiration for Bowie as a wonderful and noble man.   J. H. B.

DALLAS, TEXAS, August 19, 1881.

COLONEL GUSTAVE COOK.

HOUSTON.

GUSTAVE COOK was born in Lowndes county, Alabama, July 3, 1835. Nathaniel Cook, his father, was a native of South Carolina, for twenty-five years judge of a circuit court in Alabama, a planter and slaveholder. His mother, Harriet Anthony Herbert, was the daughter of Thomas Herbert and Elizabeth Hampton, of South Carolina. His father and mother were cousins, his paternal grandmother being Ellen Hampton, daughter of Captain Hampton, who figured at King's Mountain, in South Carolina, during the Revolution. The family are related to Senator Wade Hampton. His father is living with him at Houston, aged eighty-two. By both mother and

father, he is related to General Phil Cook, now member of congress from Georgia, and to Colonel Hillary A. Herbert now member of congress from Alabama. Walter, his oldest brother, was captain of a company in the Confederate service, and was killed at Chancellorsville, in 1863. Girard, another brother, now a prominent lawyer in Lowndes county, Alabama, was a captain in the Confederate army, in General Rhodes' brigade.

Gustave Cook was not a studious boy, and was little inclined to either schools or books. At the age of fifteen he went to Texas alone, and had neither friend nor acquaintance west of the Mississippi river. His uncle, James R. Cook, was an officer in the Texas war for independence, and was killed in the service, in 1836. His uncle's history induced Gustave to gratify his adventurous spirit by visiting the Lone Star State, and his object was to be a soldier. He arrived in the state without money, but soon made acquaintances. Among these were Three-Legged Willie, Ben McCulloch, Lamar, Burnet, Sherman, the Baylors and Burlesons, with whom he became familiar and whom he adopted as models. He grew up with the pioneer Texians and imbibed their spirit and daring.

At the age of eighteen, July 13, 1853, he married Miss Eliza Jones, daughter of Captain Randall Jones, a Texas veteran, of Fort Bend county. She was born in that county, in 1835. Her mother, Mary Andrus, was of a French family that moved from Louisiana to Texas about 1825. Four children were born of this marriage: Ida, born June 20, 1854, was educated at Mobile, and married, in Houston, January 27. 1880, Edwin Kyle, grandson of General Edward Burleson; Mary Herbert, born November 4, 1856, and educated in Houston; Henrietta, born March 13, 1859, educated in Houston; Gustave, born January 24, 1867, destined for fine stock farming.

After his marriage, Mr. Cook educated himself. The text-books employed were a spelling book, Colburn's Arithmetic, Hedges' Logic, and a Webster's Unabridged Dictionary. His favorite reading was the Spectator, the Federalist, Gibbon's Rome and Thiers' History of the French Revolution. The favorite poets of the young benedictine student were Scott and Burns. Under the advice of friends, he began reading law, in 1854, without a preceptor. But Judge John B. Jones kindly directed his legal studies, and he was admitted to the bar in 1855, and practiced in the old Austin Colony district until the beginning of the civil war.

In 1861 he enlisted as a private in the Texas army, and was under Van Dorn in the capture of Federal troops and stores in that state. In the same year he became a private in Terry's Texas Rangers, (8th Confederate cavalry,) and in this regiment was promoted successively to be sergeant, captain, major, lieutenant-colonel and colonel. He joined General Albert Sidney Johnston at Bowling Green, Kentucky, and remained with the army of Tennessee up to the surrender, in 1865, and was with his regiment in over two hundred engagements; among them, Woodsonville, Shiloh, Perryville, Murfreesboro, Chickamauga, Resaca, Marietta, Atlanta, Smithville, North Carolina, and Bentonville, in the same state. At Shiloh his right leg was broken by a musket ball; at Farmington, Tennessee, he was shot through the right arm and received a shot through the right hand that mashed every bone in it and has disfigured and almost totally disabled it; at Buckhead Church, Georgia, he was wounded by a Minnie ball through the right ankle, and at Bentonville he was shot through the right shoulder, the ball lodging in the rear of the lungs. Col. Cook received six or seven wounds during the war, and the scars he wears tell a tale of courage and gallantry and heroism far more eloquent than the praise of his biographer. He had voted for secession, and offered his life, if need were, to secure it.

When Colonel Cook reached home at the close of the conflict, in 1865, he was a mere wreck, weighing only a hundred and eighteen pounds. Broken down in health, he was also bleeding from his wounds every hour of the day. Nor was this all; he was ruined in fortune and was involved in an enormous debt, and he immediately prepared to retrieve the one and discharge the other, though the latter alone required fourteen years. Colonel Cook resumed the practice of law at his old home, and continued there until his removal to Houston, in 1870, where he has since resided. In 1874 he was by Governor Coke appointed judge of the criminal court for the district of Galveston and Harris counties, which position, by reappointment of Governor Hubbard, he has ever since held.

Before Colonel Cook was twenty-one years of age, he was clerk of the district court of Fort Bend county for nearly a year. In 1856 he was elected judge of the county court of Fort Bend, and served two years. It was after holding these offices that he began the practice of law as a separate business and a sole means of maintenance. In 1872 he was elected a member of the thirteenth legislature of Texas. He has been a delegate from Harris county to every Democratic state convention up to the time of his assuming the duties of judge. He was a delegate to the Democratic state convention at Galveston in 1876, and opposed any action on the part of the convention looking to the endorsement of the constitution then about to be submitted to the people. He was a delegate from Texas to the Philadelphia Peace Convention, in 1866. In politics, he has always been a Democrat of the states rights school, voted for secession, and favored the reconstruction policy of President Johnson. In the legislature, he opposed the land grant to the Texas and Pacific Railway Company.

Judge Cook is a worthy member of the Episcopal church, with decided tendencies to the Catholic faith, which his wife and two children have embraced. His eventful life and his frequent and almost miraculous escapes from death have attracted his attention to his relations to Deity and the dispensations of Providence toward him. He makes no concealment of his devout gratitude to God for past preservation and present prosperity. The controlling principle of his life has been to do justice, love mercy, and walk humbly before God. From his mother, a woman of exquisite beauty both of person and character, he learned to value truth and hate deceit. She taught him his religious duty, which he has never neglected. He is a devout and just man in every relation of life.

Judge Cook is a Royal Arch Mason, and honors and practices the rules of the order. As an orator, he has but few equals in Texas, and as a jurist, no superior. His legal opinions are eagerly sought and highly prized. His charges to juries are brief, concise, clear, and embrace the legal points on which they are to decide. Dignity, uprightness and absolute justice characterize his actions on the bench. In social life, he is very approachable, courtesy and affability being leading features of his admirable character. As an evidence of his legal learning and acumen, it can be truthfully affirmed that his decisions are always sustained and his judgments affirmed by the court of appeals, when appeals have been prosecuted. Since his appointment in 1874, but three of his cases have been reversed on appeal, and each of these on minor technical grounds. His knowledge is very extensive and his friends denominate him a living encyclopedia.

Judge Cook is the opposite of avaricious. His opportunities to amass wealth have been excellent, but his boundless generosity and his indifference to the accumulation of riches have forbidden him to become wealthy. He regards property as a trust by the Creator, to be used in the relief of distress and in making others comfortable, rather than in the gratification of individual lusts and appetites. His daughter, Miss Henrietta, is the financier of the family, managing the home business and directing the expenditures. He has a handsome cottage residence in Houston and a summer home in San Marcos, and besides owns several thousand acres of unimproved lands in Brown, Nueces and Hays counties, Texas. When young Cook first came to Texas, his idea, as

already intimated, was to take part in some of the numerous revolutions of Mexico, the leaders of which had their resorts along the Rio Grande, on the Texas border. These were lawless convulsions, the true nature of which he, being a youth of fifteen, did not clearly understand. But he sought counsel from those older and wiser than himself, and he was soon convinced that they presented no legitimate field for chivalric deeds and heroic achievements. Not reluctantly, therefore, he abandoned the idea of joining in these spasmodic upheavals and predatory revolutions. For two or three years he clerked in a drug store and became proficient in that line of business. This was the turning point in his life, and from the date of his abandonment of the boyish desire for adventure he began a life of usefulness, which is now crowned with honor. His aspirations since then have been to accomplish something in civil life worthy of his talents and of those relations he sustained to society. Excessively modest, and scarcely yet realizing that he has grown to manhood, he has achieved distinction without intrigue, and a high standing in public estimation without compromising his self-respect. He is justly regarded by his friends as a model of propriety, an honorable, useful and meritorious member of society.

COLONEL THOMAS JEFFERSON WARD.

PALESTINE.

THE subject of this sketch was born in Mount Airy, Surry county, North Carolina, on the 6th of February, 1805. His father was Colonel Thomas Adams Ward, a native of Charlotte county, Virginia, a land surveyor, of good education, who inherited a fine estate, but left little to his children. The father of Thomas A., Captain Charles Ward, fell a martyr to liberty at the head of his company at the glorious battle of King's Mountain, South Carolina, October 9, 1780. The mother of Colonel Thomas J. Ward was Justiana, daughter of James and Jane Dickinson, of Scotch-Irish descent. Justiana was born in Patrick county, Virginia, in 1755. Colonel Ward's father was a kinsman of President John Adams, the successor of Washington; but when he was in congress with Ex-President John Quincy Adams, in the absence of their family Bibles and records, they were unable to determine the exact degree of kinship. The Dickenson family furnished a number of prominent men in Virginia.

Colonel Ward received but a limited education. In youth he was a store clerk, a school teacher, and then for three years a law student, and in due course admitted to the bar. In 1832 he was elected to represent his native county (Surry) in the legislature, and in the same year was colonel of militia.

Having removed to Holly Springs, Mississippi, his name became famous from 1837 to 1839 by a contest for seats in the United States congress. Claibourne

and Gholson, Democrats, in August, 1837, had been elected by a general ticket to a called session of congress, and claimed seats for a full term. In November of that year the celebrated orator, Sargent S. Prentiss, and Colonel Ward, both Whigs, were elected for a full term and claimed their seats. After a full discussion, in which, by the permission of the house, Prentiss made one of his grandest oratorical efforts—a speech that made his name national—the house referred the matter back to the people of Mississippi for a new election. Prentiss and Ward re-entered the field. Gholson declined, and his place was filled by James Davis, afterwards of Texas and commander of a body of volunteers at Lipantitlan, west of the Neuces, in a battle against the Mexicans under General Canales, in June, 1842. General Davis was afterwards a member of the Texas senate, and was the father of Captain A. J. (Jack) Davis, a former citizen of Tyler and Cleburne, but now of west Texas. Prentiss and Ward were elected over Claiborne and Davis, and served out the unexpired term of the twenty-fifth congress. Colonel Ward then ranked as a states rights Whig, and in later years, on the demise of his party, consistently and naturally became a states rights Democrat, where he has ever since stood as immovable, figuratively speaking, as the rock of ages.

Colonel Ward has been married three times. His first wife, united to him in 1887, at Holly Springs, soldier, always at his post of duty and was wounded March 8, 1864, at the battle of Mansfield. In 1873 he was elected city marshal of Marshall, on the Democratic ticket. He is a Royal Arch Mason, a Knight of Pythias, a Knight of Honor and an Odd Fellow. He is a man who is genial, generous and kind: a good citizen and a warm friend.

Dudley Smith Jennings, jr., was born November 15, 1847, in Jackson, Mississippi, came with his parents to Texas, and was married November 17, 1873, to Miss Carrie M., daughter of Josiah Marshall, deceased, of Marshall, Texas. They have one child, a son named Marshall, born November 14, 1876. Mr. Jennings is an Odd Fellow and a member of the order of United Workmen. He is located at Longview, Texas, where he practices law and has served as mayor and justice of the peace for several years. Politically, he is a Democrat, religiously, a Baptist.

Robertus Love Jennings, the business manager of the firm of Jennings Brothers, was born in Jackson, Mississippi, October 18, 1849. He is emphatically the carver of his own fortunes; having risen to positions of trust and honorable responsibility from humble beginnings. He is almost exclusively a business man, is possessed of fine administrative abilities and indomitable energy. He has a most generous disposition, his heart is full of kindly impulses and he never fails his friends in any emergency. He is a Master Mason, a Knight of Honor, a United Workman, in which order he has passed all the chairs, an ex-chief of the Marshall fire department, and was elected alderman by the Democrats in 1868. He married Miss Susan Belle, daughter of John H. Duke, of Red River county, Texas, December 29, 1869, and they have three children: Robertus, born May 30, 1871; Mary Susan, born August 4, 1877, and Rowley William, born December 21, 1880.

Mrs. Jennings is earnest in all good works, an affectionate wife and mother, a woman of natural grace and refinement of maner, a capable house keeper and domestic in all her tastes. Mr. Jennings attributes his success in life to the helping hand of his judicious wife.

John Alexander Jennings was born in Harrison county, Texas, July 18, 1853. He is numbered among the substantial business men of Longview, Texas, where he is engaged in the drug business. He is a Master Mason and a member of the American Legion of Honor.

James Johnson Jennings, the junior member of the firm of Jennings Brothers and foreman of the printing department of their publishing house, was born in Harrison county, Texas, February 12, 1856. He is a modest, unassuming gentleman, whose sterling worth, promptness and faithfulness will insure success in whatever department of life his energies may be called forth.

The name of Hon. Dudley Smith Jennings stands pre-eminent among the lawyers of his day. He stood in the front rank of his profession. Educated in a school where patient investigation and careful analysis were required, where he must measure strength with men who had a national reputation, he attained a high degree of intellectual excellence. He was a logical reasoner and sought to fathom the philosophy of law. As a public speaker he commanded attention by his candor, sincerity of manner and real ability. His style was marked by its chastity, felicity of diction, clearness, directness and force, added to which was a commanding presence and a dignified bearing.

A leading lawyer says of Judge Jennings:

As a jurist, he was one of the great men of the state and the South; and his talents were never so conspicuous as when forced to the highest mental effort by formidable opposition. He belonged to that class of intellectual men who go to the bottom of all questions, and exhaust the subjects they investigate and discuss. He was a representative man of that class, of which our free institutions have presented so many brilliant examples.

Wedded to his profession, he esteemed its honors as sufficient reward, and, refusing political preferment, established a reputation which was in itself a distinguished honor. Generous in his disposition, intellectual in his tastes, philanthropic in his life, he dedicated himself, with a singleness of aim and a fidelity of purpose, to a life which enlisted all the talents of his educated manhood. Socially he was a genial companion, devoted to his friends and his family, and in all the relations of life a noble man.

HON. THOMAS J. JENNINGS.

FORT WORTH.

THE subject of this sketch was born in Shenandoah county, Virginia, on the 20th of October, 1801. His parents were Colonel William Jennings and Marian Howard Smith. Colonel Jennings, for a number of years, was sheriff of the county, was a man of fine social qualities and universally esteemed.

When the subject of this sketch was about ten years old his father moved to Indiana, where he purchased five thousand acres of land at a point on the Ohio

river near Vevay. He remained there but a short time, when he moved to Louisville, Kentucky, and purchased a large portion of the land upon which the city is located, which he afterwards sold for a sum which at this day appears insignificant.

After a short residence at Louisville, Colonel Jennings removed to Christian county, in that state, where Thomas J. Jennings was engaged in clerking in a country store and going to school until he was about seventeen years old, when he commenced teaching school. After teaching two or three years he accumulated sufficient means to attend Transylvania College, at Lexington, Kentucky, where he graduated, in 1824, with the highest honors, having been selected by his classmates to deliver the valedictory. Jefferson Davis, late president of the Confederacy, Gustavus H. Henry, of Tennessee, and a number of other men that afterwards became distinguished in law, medicine, politics and the ministry, were his classmates. The love he acquired for the classics at Transylvania College clung to him through life, and he never lost an opportunity to cultivate them. There was, perhaps, no more accurate or critical Latin and Greek scholar in the South, but his acquirements were not confined to Greek and Latin, for he was thoroughly familiar with the French and Spanish languages, speaking them both with the ease and fluency that he did his own vernacular. After graduating he taught school a short time at Paris, Tennessee, studying law at the same time. Soon after being admitted to the bar, he went into partnership with his brother, Dudley S. Jennings, and they practised at Paris about two years, when they dissolved partnership and the subject of our sketch commenced practicing at Huntington, Tennessee, in partnership with Berry Gillespie. In 1836 he went to Yazoo City, Mississippi, and did a large and lucrative practice there until the spring of 1840, when he moved to Texas, first settling at San Augustine, remaining there until the fall of that year, when he went to Nacogdoches.

In January, 1844, he married at that place Mrs. Sarah G. Mason, the only daughter of Major Hyde, a prominent citizen of Nacogdoches and formerly a leading merchant in Nashville, Tennessee. Mrs. Mason was highly educated, had been raised with great care and tenderness, was a lady of excellent sense, of rare literary attainments and universally admired for those qualities which adorn her sex.

While residing at Nacogdoches he was in partnership, successively, with J. M. Ardrey and W. B. Ochiltree, both of whom were eminent lawyers in their day and time.

In 1852 he was elected attorney-general, and on the expiration of his term, in 1852, was re-elected and held that position till 1856, when he declined a re-election.

In 1856 he removed to his plantatation, near Alto, in Cherokee county, Texas.

In 1857 he was elected to the legislature from Cherokee county. In 1861 he was elected to the convention that passed the ordinance of seccession. In the fall of 1861 he had a stroke of paralysis, which confined him to his bed eighteen months, and he never in after life recovered from the effects of it.

In the fall of 1864 he removed to Tyler and went into partnership with B. T. Selman. In 1868, having dissolved partnership with Colonel Selman, he and his son, Tom R. Jennings, formed a partnership. Colonel Jennings continued actively in the practice until 1875, when, owing to his advanced years and

failing health, he retired from the practice, having practiced law steadily and uninterruptedly for half a century. He had, at different times, been in partnership with George F. Moore, late chief-justice of the supreme court; Stockton P. Donley and Reuben H. Reeves, late associate justices of the supreme court.

In 1877 he removed to Fort Worth, Texas, where he died, after a long and painful illness, September 23, 1881. He had three sons: Tom R., Monroe D. and Hyde Jennings. His oldest son, Tom R. Jennings, is practicing law at Nacogdoches, Texas. Monroe D. died when nineteen years old, at Alto, in Cherokee county, in September, 1868. His youngest son, Hyde Jennings, is a leading lawyer at Fort Worth. His faithful wife resides with her son, Hyde, at the same place.

Colonel Jennings was a Mason and Odd Fellow, and, while not a member of any particular church, lead an honorable life, conspicuous for its virtues.

Among the public men that have adorned the history of Texas, there was not one that possessed in a more marked degree those qualities of mind and heart that challenge admiration. In his investigations he was untiring. He mastered every question he endeavored to discuss. His speeches were clear, forcible and logical, and when he concluded the court and jury were impressed with the conviction that he had exhausted the subject as viewed from his standpoint. Socially, he was amiable, kind and generous to a fault. He was brave, high-toned and honorable, loving virtue for itself. His sense of justice, liberality and kindly feeling were displayed in his regard for others. Of this the writer of this sketch had an example in 1857. Colonel Jennings was then a member of the legislature, and, upon being drawn out as to his opinion of the leading men of the state, took them up, seriatam, dwelling upon the excellent qualities—mentally, morally and socially—of each. Such a thing as jealous rivalry never had a place in his mind, and he was never known to speak disparagingly of any one. As a man, he possessed those qualities which endeared him to every one; as a jurist, he was able and profound, and, as a politician, he was patriotic. Few men were as well informed in regard to public affairs, and none more useful and generous in the discharge of every duty. Public welfare always found in Colonel Jennings a friend. He was a friend to the friendless, a helper of the needy. As a man with the best interests of his community at heart, he was ever ready with his purse and his influence to assist whatever project was inaugurated calculated to help the masses, and it is but natural that such a man must ever be missed by those who knew him best. The task of writing a fitting memoir of one who, for so long a time figured conspicuously in all the affairs of interest to Texas and the general government, is not an easy one, and in the foregoing sketch of the life of one of the noblest sons ever born unto Texas, it has been intended to give only that part of Colonel Jennings' history that will prove useful to the future generations of men. This book is not wanting in information from which those intending to make the science of the law a study, can glean useful points to shape their course of life by; so, also, may the young merchant, needing some life that has been a success in its career to fashion his own by, come to these pages and draw all the inspiration his imagination may require. This is a work written and published with this object in view—to educate the future. "The lives of great men all remind us" that we of to-day should do something to be remembered by the young and old of to-morrow, and this effort has been made in the production of the Encyclopedia of the lives of the men and women of the present generation.

GENERAL THOMAS J. RUSK.

NACOGDOCHES.

I HAVE been requested by the publishers of THE ENCYCLOPEDIA OF THE NEW WEST to write a sketch of one of the most distinguished citizens Texas ever had, and one of the most elegant men and sincere patriots that ever sat in the American senate. The duty is encompassed with difficulties, from the fact that I never lived in the locality of General Rusk, know little of his genealogy and only knew him through his admirable career as a citizen, a soldier and statesman of Texas.

This, however, is known, that he was born in South Carolina, in Pendleton district, December 5, 1803, the son of a worthy Irish stone-mason—that he early attracted the attention of John C. Calhoun, under whose counsels he was educated and studied law. He then settled in Georgia, stepped at once to the head of the bar, married an accomplished daughter of General Cleveland and came to Nacogdoches, Texas, in the winter of 1834-35. Then as now, the people of Texas cared not whence a man came nor how long he had been here, in the estimation of his mind and worth.

No people under the sun have ever existed more generous and liberal in regard to length of residence or nationality in birth, in the judgment of men, than the people of Texas, from its Anglo Saxon birth in 1821 to date. Compared with the early settlers of New England, Virginia, Pennsylvania and Maryland, the contrast is so great as to demand the verdict of impartial philosophy in its solution. Old Texians are proud of the fact, but have no theory for its solution. They instinctively know it as a truth and behold nothing strange in it. They—the real Texians—are unaware that it is peculiar and distinctive. It is only appreciated by the ever-incoming tide of immigrants and travelers. But that it is a fact, none who have a right by observation to judge, will deny. Hundreds of illustrations could be given strikingly demonstrative of the fact, but space forbids.

Rusk, a young man of tall and commanding presence, of dark complexion, tinged with a roseate hue, of deep set and benevolent eyes, manly and kindly features, beaming with nobility of soul, came to Nacogdoches a young stranger in search of a home and fortune but a little before the relations of Texas to Mexico assumed portentous shape. A single glance at his splendid presence won every heart, and the whole people took him on trust. While yet a stranger, unknown to himself and alone by the instinct of the old municipality of Nacogdoches, he was a leader of the people on the doorstep of a bloody revolution.

The convention which declared Texas an independent Republic, met at Washington, on the Brazos, March 1, 1836, Rusk was there as a delegate from Nacogdoches and his name is affixed to the declaration. Thence, till his death in 1857, his history is so much of the history of Texas, and inseparable from it.

By David G. Burnet, the president *ad interim* from March to October, 1836, he was made secretary of war; but chanced to be in and win laurels at the battle of San Jacinto. When General Houston retired early in May, in search of medical treatment in New Orleans, Rusk was made commander-in-chief of the army, and, at its head, followed the retreating Mexicans to Goliad. There he called a halt—caused the bones of Fannin's four hundred and eighty massacred men to be collected and interred, and over their grave delivered an address which moistened the cheeks of every man in that motley group of half-naked, half-starved and illy-armed volunteer soldiery.

For a few months he remained in command of the army; then returned to his home in Nacogdoches, where he was elected to the first congress of the newly-born Republic. By that body he was elected a brigadier-general of the Republic and as such in October, 1838, fought and defeated a large body of Indians at the Kickapoo village in East Texas.

In July, 1839, he commanded a portion of the troops in the Cherokee battles of July 16 and 17. In the same year he was elected by congress chief justice of the supreme court of the Republic and held the first term at Austin in the winter of 1839-40. Under the Republic the chief justice and the district judges composed the supreme court. He held the position for a time—then resigned and devoted himself to the practice of law, in which he had but a single rival in East Texas, in the person of his friend, General J. Pinckney Henderson. He loved the freedom of retirement and had no taste for office-seeking or the mysticisms of political life. But in 1845, when the convention was called to form a constitution for Texas as a proposed state of the Union, General Rusk was unanimously elected a delegate from Nacogdoches. When the convention assembled on the Fourth of July he was unanimously elected its president, and when the legislature, under the new constitution, assembled on the 16th of February, 1846, he was elected by the unanimous vote of both the senate and house, to be one of the two first senators from the state of Texas to the congress of the United States, his colleague being General Sam Houston. In 1843 he had been elected major-general of the Republic.

Together, they took their seats in March, 1846—together, by the re-election of each, they sat eleven years, till the melancholy death of Rusk in 1857. Together they represented the sovereignty and defended the rights of Texas—together they shed lustre on their state—together they sustained President Polk in the prosecution of the Mexican war—together they, each for himself, declined a proffered major-generalship in the army of invasion into Mexico—together they labored to give Texas the full benefit of her mergence into the Union in regard to mail routes, frontier protection and custom house facilities—together they labored in behalf of the compromises of 1850, the adjustment of the boundary of Texas and sale (as a peace offering,) of our Northwest territory to the United States—and together they sought to encourage the construction of a transcontinental railway, on the parallel of thirty-two degrees north latitude from the Mississippi river and the Gulf of Mexico, through Texas, to the Pacific ocean—an achivement cemented in victory yesterday. December 1, 1881, twenty-four years after the death of Rusk and eighteen years after the old hero of San Jacinto closed his eventful career.

For several years General Rusk was elected to the honorable position of president pro tem. of the United States senate and presided with a dignity and impartiality that commanded the respect and esteem of every member of that body.

In 1854, with a select band of friends, he traversed Texas from east to west on the parallel of thirty-two, to see for himself the practicability of a railway route and became thoroughly satisfied of its feasibility and cheapness, as he was already of its untold blessings in the progress of civilization in America and its mighty influence on commercial intercourse between the continents of Europe and Asia. He was a wise man in his day and generation; a just man in all the relations of life; a patriot as pure as the dews of Heaven; a husband and father tender to weakness; a friend guileless and true; an orator persuasive and convincing; a soldier from a sense of duty, in battle fearless as a tiger; in peace gentle as a dove: ambitious only for an honorable name, honorably won, but regarding as dross the tinsel, display and pomp of ephemeral splendor. In a word, Thomas J. Rusk was a marked manifestation of nature's goodness in the creation of one of her noblest handiworks. When he died Texas mourned from hut to palace, for the whole people, even the slaves, wherever known to them, loved him.

Would that I could reproduce a few sentences from the eulogy upon him by that peerless son of Texas, the late Thomas M. Jack, before a weeping audience in Galveston; but my copy of it is among the treasures lost in the late war.

Fidelity to truth bids the statement—so painful to a whole commonwealth—that this noble citizen, patriot and statesman, died by his own hand, at his own home, in Nacogdoches, in the summer of 1857.

His cherished and adored wife, to whom he was not only attached with rare devotion, but for whom he had a reverence as remarkable as beautiful, had died a little before. His grief, quiet but unappeasable, superinduced melancholy. A ravenous carbuncle, at the base of the skull, racked his brain, and in a moment of temporary aberration, to the amazement of his household, his soul went hence to a merciful God.   J. H. B.

ONE HUNDRED OLD TEXIANS.

IN PREPARING the following brief notice of over a hundred persons, nearly all deceased, who figured usefully and most of them with more or less distinction in the earlier days of Texas, brevity has been demanded to the utmost extent consistent with an intelligent glance at the character of the party and the services rendered. The compend has been chiefly made from memory, which must, of necessity, be occasionally at fault. The list could be extended did space and time permit. To a considerable extent it embraces persons who have received no notice in other works, but who deserve mention in a labor of this kind. This is wholly disconnected with the regular biographical sketches otherwise appearing in THE ENCYCLOPEDIA, prepared from data furnished by others. It is a labor of love, resting upon its own merits.   J. H. B.

ARCHER, Branch T., one of the ablest, most eloquent and purest patriots Texas ever had, was born of an ancient family in Virginia, received a medical education in Philadelphia—served in the Virginia legislature as speaker of the house—came to Brazoria, Texas, in 1831, and was a master spirit in the revolution. He was president of the first general consultation (convention) in 1835, one of three commissioners with Stephen F. Austin and William H. Wharton to the United States in 1835-6—a member of the congress in 1836, and speaker at the session of 1837—secretary of war under President Lamar in 1840 and 1841, and died in the family of Mrs. William H. Wharton, in Brazoria county, September 23, 1856. He was remarkably tall, of dark complexion, deep set eyes, finely arched brows, and a man of commanding presence, distinguished as an orator and loved for the nobility of his nature. Archer county perpetuates his name. His only child, Dr. Powhatan Archer, stood high in Brazoria as a physician and gentleman and died in the Confederate army.

ANDREWS, Robert, a courageous young man of good family, the only Texian killed in the brilliant repulse of the Mexicans at the "Mission of Conception," October 28, 1835. Andrews county, adjoining the southeast corner of New Mexico, was named in his honor.

ALEXANDER, Rev. Robert, a man of six feet two, came from Tennessee, a young Methodist preacher in 1837. Of limited education, but fine presence, he grew in mental power by laborious study, and speedily became, long to remain, a pillar of the church to which he belonged, honored and respected by the members of all other denominations. As a boy of those primitive frontier days, listening to his discourses in cabins and under arbors—then meeting him in manhood—remembering his lifting me, an invalid, faint on horseback, into his buggy, during the late war and conveying me many miles to the family I had not seen in eleven eventful months, and knowing his long and useful career in the field of his labors—it is meet that he should have a place in this list of worthy benefactors, so we raise his name from its tomb of oblivion.

BAKER, Rev. Daniel, D. D., a native of Virginia, distinguished as an evangelist in the Presbyterian church, known from Pennsylvania to Texas, and one of the most remarkable pulpit orators of the country. He visited Texas when it was a Republic and made a decided impression, adding to the church numbers of men of wealth and education, their sons and daughters. He returned in 1848, becoming a citizen. He was made president of Austin College, a Presbyterian institution at Huntsville, now at Sherman. He was a remarkable man, of great power. He died on a visit to Austin in behalf of education, during the session of the legislature in the winter of 1857-8, and was buried with distinguished honors.

BOURLAND, Colonel James, came from Kentucky to Northeast Texas about 1840. He was a representative man of the intelligent and progressive Southwest—a clear-headed, frank, hospitable and very courageous man—fond of the sports peculiar to his time and section, but ever reverencing the institutions of religion and the precepts of his pious parents—one of those men who, like Bowie, seemed destined to be misunderstood and misrepresented by casual observers. He located on Red river and was sent to the first senate of the state after our annexation to the United States and served four years. Afterwards he opened a plantation, established a trading house in the horseshoe bend of Red river, in the extreme northeast corner of Cooke county, where, for many years, he established a beneficient influence over the Chickasaw Indians. When William C. Young raised a regiment for the Mexican war, of which he was elected colonel, Mr. Bourland was elected lieutenant-colonel, and his brother, William Bourland, major. But the war closed about the time they reached the

Rio Grande and they never participated in any battle. In the late civil war James Bourland commanded a regiment whose duty it was to protect the Northwestern frontier against the hostile Indians in the darkest day ever known in that region. He performed that onerous duty with a fidelity and success that saved the lives of thousands of women and children. The country was not only endangered by the forays of wild savages, but a home organization—as in South Carolina during the Revolutionary war—who sought to plunder and burn the houses of the people. Their plots were discovered and a number of the guilty hung. In after years, when Colonel Bourland was on his death-bed, a Texian paper had the indelicacy to so connect the name of Colonel Bourland with that transaction as to style him "the hangman of Texas"—a great wrong on historic truth. Space forbids a statement of the facts; but throughout that grave and solemn occasion, from first to last, the conduct of Colonel Bourland was that of a brave, conscientious man, and he saved the lives of several guilty persons, because of their youth or for the sake of their families. It was a terrible ordeal—just such as often happened in the war of 1776—and stern necessity, under the law of self-protection, demanded examples to be made; but none more than Colonel Bourland sought to limit the punishment within the narrowest possible bounds. He sleeps in an honored grave and will ever be revered by those who know his true character and career.

BOURLAND, Major William, a brother of James—the first county clerk in Holly Springs, Mississippi, came to Texas about the same time as his brother—was a representative in the first legislature of 1846, from Lamar county, and several times afterwards from Grayson—a major in Young's regiment in the Mexican war, and generally a man of sterling worth. Having married Miss Willis, an educated lady of the Chickasaw Nation, he removed into that territory, opposite the horseshoe bend of Red river, and died just before the late war. The family of Bourland is numerous in Kentucky, Tennessee, Mississippi, Missouri and Texas, and has ever stood as honorable and patriotic.

BELL, Mrs. Mary E., the young bride of Josiah H. Bell, (née Miss McKenzie), of Kentucky, arrived on the Brazos early in 1822, and, the same year, became the mother of the second child born in Austin's colony. This was in Washington. They soon settled in Brazoria county, where her second son, Hon. James H. Bell, was born. He was in the Somervell expedition, educated at Yale College, elected district judge in 1856, and to the supreme bench in 1859, the first native of the state so honored. The only other child of Mr. and Mrs. Bell became the accomplished and estimable wife of Dr. J. W. Copes. Mrs. Bell was a remarkable woman to be found in a wilderness—educated, refined and deeply imbued with religious convictions—a devoted member of the Presbyterian church. Her example and influence ever had a wholesome effect on those in the circle of her acquaintance, which, for years, covered the whole country. She assisted in founding the first Sunday-school in Texas, in 1828. Her house was the home of preachers and missionaries, without reference to their denominations, and the first men of the land were proud of her acquaintance. Through all the hardships of a wilderness life, Indian wars and the revolution, unto the day of her death, before the late war, she remained the same consistent, gentle, persuasive Christian woman. The name of her husband is inseparably and honorably connected with the history of Austin's colony, and her memory is embalmed in every loving heart whose possessor knew her.

BONNELL, George W., a native of Onondaga county, New York, a man of good education and a fluent newspaper writer. He early removed to Alabama, editing papers at Selma and Mobile, also in Columbus and Aberdeen, Mississippi. In 1836 he came to Texas—was major in the volunteer service and commanded a batallion in an Indian expedition in 1838, but had no fight. He also edited a paper in 1838-9 in Houston, and through 1840 and 1841, conducted the Texas *Sentinel* in Austin, the first number being issued in January, 1840, on which were employed Joseph A. Clark, (now of Thorp's Springs, Hood county), William Clark, (deceased in Houston about 1850), John Henry Brown, (now of Dallas), and Martin Carroll Wing, in 1843, one of the seventeen decimated Mier prisoners. The *Sentinel* was the second paper in Austin, being preceded a few weeks by the Austin *City Gazette*, owned by Samuel Whiting, and edited by George K. Teulon, an Englishman, who died in China, as an American consul. On the *Gazette* were employed Judge Joel Miner, Alexander Area, William B. McClelland, W. D. Mims and other printers. Major Bonnell was a chivalrous, impetuous man, of small, lithe stature, red hair and sparkling gray eyes—unselfish, generous and loved by his associates. He was on a commission, early in 1839, to the hostile Comanches, high up the Colorado. He also wrote a small volume, now out of print, descriptive of Texas. In 1842 he joined the Somervell expedition—was one of the guard on the east bank of the river, when the Texians surrendered in Mier, and, with a Mr. Hicks, was the last to seek safety in flight, waiting till the last moment to assist across the river any who may have escaped. They left only on the appearance of Mexican cavalry on the opposite side; but were captured ten miles out and carried back. Reaching the river at twilight, Hicks escaped into the chapparel, and finally reached home and made this statement to the writer of this. That was the last ever heard of Major Bonnell, who was doubtless killed on the escape of Hicks. In his honor, in 1838, General Edward Burleson bestowed the name (yet retained) of Bonnell on the now pleasant resort and beautiful mount four miles above Austin. He had no kindred in Texas, but is fondly remembered by many who knew his worth and his intense patriotism.

BURNET, David Gouveneur, was born in Newark, New Jersey, the youngest son of Dr. William Burnet, April 4, 1789—received a superior education, served as a lieutenant in the Miranda expedition to South

America in 1806—spent nearly two years in 1817-18 with the Comanche Indians in Texas—made his home in Texas in 1826—served in the convention of 1833-- was elected the first president *ad interim* of the Republic, serving from March 18 to October 22, 1836; elected vice-president, serving from December, 1838, to December, 1834, part of the time acting as president. His last public service was as secretary of state under the first governor. J. P. Henderson, in 1846-7. He was preceded to the grave by his noble wife and all of his children, his last son, as a Confederate major, being killed in the battle of Mobile. He died in Galveston, in 1871, honored by all Texas. He was elected to the United States congress in 1866, but not allowed to take his seat. Under the Mexican government he was a district judge. In politics he was simply a Texian—in religion, by inheritance and practical life, a Presbyterian. Burnet county perpetuates his name in the geography of the state.

BONHAM, James Butler, a heroic son of South Carolina, forever linked with the history of Texas, from having entered the Alamo, seven days after the siege began, with a detachment of thirty-two men from Gonzales, each of whom added one to the list of immolated martyrs. Bonham, in Fannin county, was named for him at its birth about 1838-9.

BROWN, Captain Jeremiah, an officer of the Texian navy, a native of the North, who won a strong hold on the people of Texas. He lived at Brazoria.

BROWN, Captain William, a brother of the foregoing, a brave naval officer.

BROWN, Colonel Reuben R., a Georgian, one of the few who escaped from the massacre in the Johnson and Grant expedition upon Patricio, in the winter of 1835-6—a brave and intelligent man, who settled at the mouth of the Brazos after the revolution, and was a colonel in the Confederate army during the late war.

BROWN, George William, a brilliant young lawyer from Henrico county, Virginia, who settled at Columbus, was United States district attorney, a member of the convention of 1845, and died of consumption in the dawning of a brilliant career in 1847.

BROWN, Captain Henry S., born in Madison county, Kentucky, March 8, 1793, (six days after the birth of Sam Houston, in Rockbridge county, Virginia), went to Missouri in 1810, was a soldier in the war of 1812-15, came to Texas in 1824, was a soldier and often a captain on the Indian frontier, a captain at Velasco, June 26, 1832, and died in Columbia, Brazonia county, July 26, 1834. The first congress of Texas held its session in a house built and owned by Captain Brown, and in which he died. Brown county, created in 1856, twenty-two years after his death, was named for him.

BROWN, John, (known in his day as Waco Brown), born in Madison county, Kentucky, came to Texas with his brother, Henry S., in 1824, was captured by the Waco Indians, in the spring of 1825, escaped from them in August, 1826, met his brother Henry at San Felipe, who pursued the band from which he escaped, and killed sixteen of the seventeen Indians composing the party, on the head of Cummins creek, in what is now Fayette county. Subsequently John settled as a merchant in partnership with Captain Philip Dimmitt, in San Antonio, and died there December 8, 1831.

BROWN, Dr. Caleb S., brother of Captain Henry S. and John, born in Madison county, Kentucky, in 1805, came to Gonzales, from Mississippi, in May, 1840, was surgeon at the battle of Plum creek, August 12, 1840, and Salado, September 18, 1841—a lion-hearted man in danger, gentle as a lamb in peace—noble, generous and benevolent. He died in February, 1855, leaving a widow and one infant daughter.

BROWN, Captain Nicholas, half-brother of the three preceding, born in Madison county, Kentucky, left motherless in infancy, came to Texas from Mississippi, captain of a company of volunteers in 1836, afterwards a merchant at Rodney, Mississippi, returned to Texas in 1847, commanded an overland company to California in 1849, commanded in a fight with the Indians on the Stanislaus river, in the winter of 1849-50, accumulated a fortune in mercantile pursuits at Stockton, was burnt out, losing eighty thousand dollars, and again returned to Gonzales, Texas. He died of yellow fever, on a business trip to Brownsville, in 1864, leaving no descendant—a modest, honest and brave man, named for an older half-brother, who was killed in Dudley's defeat, opposite Fort Meigs, in 1813.

BUCHEL, Colonel Augustus, a native of Prussia, educated in military schools, was a lieutenant in the Prussian army but resigned, served in the armies of Turkey and Spain, and arrived, still a young man, in Indianola, Texas, in 1845. He commanded a three months' company under General Taylor, in Mexico, in 1846, which, being discharged, he served with distinction on General Taylor's staff at Buena Vista. He commanded a splendid Texas regiment in the Confederate army, rose rapidly in public favor, and fell in a desperate charge at the head of his regiment at Mansfield, in April, 1864, deplored by the whole army. He was interred, with marked honors, in the state cemetery at Austin. He was a man of remarkable polish, extreme modesty, and as noble as he was brave.

BLAIR, Rev. William C., a native of Ohio, and a soldier throughout the war of 1812-15, long resident near Natchez, Mississippi, where he married, came to Victoria, Texas, a missionary of the Presbyterian church, in 1839. He was a preacher for fifty years—a man of superior mind and education. He was prominently identified with the struggles of his church, especially in Southwest Texas, till his death in Port Lavaca, in 1872, when about eighty-five years of age. He was a man of singularly happy endowments in social and domestic life, given to generous hospitality and always an instructive conversationalist. His widow died in Lexington, Kentucky, September 7, 1881.

BABBITT, General Edwin B., United States army. Though never a citizen of Texas, this honored and revered gentleman and soldier, was so long on duty in our state, and so endeared to our people wherever known, that he deserves a place in this connection. He was a native of Massachusetts, as was his noble and beloved wife, who was a sister of General Sprague,

of the United States army. He was long stationed as quartermaster, first at San Antonio, and then for several years at Indianola, whence, before the war, he was transferred to Baltimore, and thence to the Pacific coast. Since being on the retired list, he resided in Portland, Oregon, where he died in 1880. He was, in the highest sense, a religious man, devoted to good deeds, conscientious, dignified and exceedingly affable, and his family were worthy of such a husband and father. His eldest daughter, Fanny, became the widow of Lieutenant Barber, a few weeks after marriage in Indianola. Laura, is the wife of Colonel ———, of the army, and her twin-brother, Lawrence, is an officer in the same. Though a thorough Union man, General Babbitt stood ready to renew his old Southern friendships as soon as the last gun was fired.

BUNTON, John W., came from Tennessee to Texas, in 1833, landed in Brazoria, settled at Bastrop, signed the declaration of independence, was a soldier of San Jacinto, a member of congress in 1836 and 1837, served in numerous expeditions against the Indians, finally settled in Hayes county where he died three or four years ago, leaving a handsome estate.

CARL, Rev. Daniel, a Methodist preacher from Tennessee, in 1837, long labored on the frontier and served in several Indian and Mexican campaigns as a soldier, noted for coolness, courage and a high sense of duty, always respected and esteemed, even by the wildest young men of the border. He was a welcome guest in every household, regardless of creed, and exercised a wide and beneficial influence till retired from ill-health. He was a man of strong, logical mind, and at times reached the higher plane of oratory. He died at his home in Victoria county, (possibly in the edge of De Witt), several years ago, leaving a widow and several children.

CALLAHAN, Captain James H., a Georgian, one of the few who escaped from Fannin's massacre, long a brave defender of the frontier and in many fights. He commanded a company in the retreat from San Antonio, March 6, 1842, another in the battle of Salado, September 18, 1842, and led three companies in October, 1855, across the Rio Grande, in pursuit of the Kickapoo Indians, who had been depredating in Texas. A bloody fight occurred near San Fernando, in which he was confronted by superior numbers, but succeeded in falling back and recrossing the river. His bearing commanded the warmest commendation of his men, made up of the most daring spirits of the Southwest. He long resided in Seguin, but died in Hayes county, in 1856. Callahan county was named in his honor.

CALDER, Robert J., came from Maryland in 1832, commanded a company at San Jacinto, has been sheriff and county judge of Fort Bend county, where he still resides, a planter and a man honored and respected for the attributes of a gentleman, a soldier and a good citizen.

CHALK, Whitfield, a North Carolinian, who came to Texas in 1839. He, and a man named St. Clair, were the only ones who escaped at the time of the surrender at Mier, Christmas day, 1842. In the confusion they burrowed under a pile of ground sugar cane, in a back yard, remained till night and succeeded, with great suffering for food and sore of foot, in reaching Texas. A quiet, honest man, now residing at Lampasas. His brother, Ira W. Chalk, is a Methodist preacher.

COLEMAN, Captain Robert M., a native of Christian county, Kentucky, a man of courage and enterprise, settled at Bastrop, on the Colorado, about 1830, and was in numerous campaigns against the Indians—a captain in 1835, against the Tehuacanos, under Colonel John H. Moore, and a captain at San Jacinto. He also signed the declaration of independence. He was drowned in the mouth of the Brazos in 1837. His home, in Webber's prairie, above Bastrop, was attacked by a large body of Indians in 1838, and heroically defended by his widow and a son of thirteen years, both of whom were killed and a smaller son carried into captivity never to be recovered. Two little girls, secreted by their mother under the puncheon floor, were rescued the night following by the brave and afterwards eloquent and distinguished young lawyer, John D. Anderson, who served in the constitutional convention in 1845, and died in Guadalupe county in 1848. Coleman county was named as a memorial of this valiant pioneer.

CLAY, Nestor, an early immigrant from Kentucky, a man of splendid talent, who won distinction among giants in the provincial convention of 1833, and died before the revolution of 1836. His brother, Tacitus, and kindred resided, and the survivors yet reside, in Washington county. He was a cousin of the brothers Sidney, Cassius M. and Brutus J. Clay, of Kentucky, and a second cousin of the great statesman, Henry Clay.

CALDWELL, Colonel Matthew, (commonly called "Old Paint," from the spotted color of his whiskers), came early from Kentucky, where he was born in 1798, to DeWitt's colony, and at once became a prominent defender of the frontier. He was in a fight with the Indians at the head of the San Marcos in the spring of 1835. He was a soldier in 1835-6, a quartermaster part of the time. He signed the declaration of independence. He was a captain in the regular army from 1838 to 1841; but commanded one wing of the citizen volunteers at the battle of Plum creek, August 12, 1840. In 1841 he was a captain in the celebrated Santa Fe expedition, which was betrayed and captured near Santa Fe, imprisoned in the City of Mexico about a year and released. He reached home barely in time to be elected colonel commanding the citizen volunteers in the victorious battle of Salado, September 18, 1842—two hundred and two Texians against one thousand four hundred Mexicans. He died at his old Gonzales home in January, 1843, lamented as one of the noblest patriots of the country. Caldwell county was named for him.

CALDWELL, Colonel Pinkney, was a soldier of repute in the revolution and a man of talent. He was killed by the Indians in their raid on Victoria, August 7, 1840.

CALDWELL, John, came from Tennessee to the Colorado in 1830. He became a wealthy planter and was long in public life. He entered congress in 1838 and was many years a senator—a man of fine, practical sense and irreproachable character. He died a few years since, leaving a large estate and numerous family.

COCKE, James D., a lawyer and printer, from Richmond, Virginia, gallant and chivalrous, a Mier prisoner, who drew a black bean in the lottery of life as a Mier prisoner, and was shot to death by the famous order of Santa Anna, in April, 1843.

COOKE, James R., one of the bravest of the brave, of Tennessee lineage, but from Alabama to Texas, a cavalry lieutenant at San Jacinto, a daring soldier on the Indian frontier, and a colonel in the Somervell expedition to the Rio Grande in 1842. On horseback one of the finest looking men Texas ever had, in person of commanding presence. In heart, one of the noblest of men. In voice, in battle array, a second Roderick Dhu. A man of the forest, loved and honored for the chivalry and nobility of his nature. He lost his life in a personal difficulty about the last days of March or the first of April, 1843, deplored by a whole commonwealth.

COOKE, William G., a druggist from Richmond, Virginia, to New Orleans, whence, in 1835, he came to Texas as lieutenant of the New Orleans Grays, the first company that ever came from the United States to the relief of Texas. He was at the storming of San Antonio, afterwards quartermaster-general of the Republic, in 1841 a commissioner in the ill-fated Santa Fe expedition—long imprisoned in Mexico—on the staff of General Somervell in 1842, married an accomplished young daughter of Don Luciano Navarro, and died in 1847. Cooke county is named for him.

COOKE, Louis P., born in Tennessee, entered West Point Military Academy—expelled before graduation—came to Texas from New York in the Morehouse expedition, arriving just in time to miss the battle of San Jacinto; lieutenant-colonel in the army of 1836-37, member of congress from Brazoria in 1838-39, secretary of the navy under President Lamar from 1839 to 1841, a wild, courageous and somewhat reckless man, had an eye shot out by an Indian arrow near Corpus Christi in 1845, and died of cholera at Brownsville in 1849. His brother, Dr. Wilds K. Cooke, was a senator from the Robertson district, in the first legislature after annexation; and another brother, H. W. Cooke, of Coryell, was a captain on the frontier in 1859. Louis P. Cooke was an extraordinary man. His history, life and death abound in romance, a romance of courageous recklessness, clouded by actions in contrast with his otherwise admirable character.

COTTLE, George Washington, one of a large family who came from Lincoln county, Missouri, to Gonzales, Texas, between 1826 and 1830. His head-right league covers the head spring of the Lavaca river, on or near which is the new railroad of Flatonia. He entered the Alamo during the siege, with the chivalrous Bonham, and there lost his life to his country, for which, forty years later, his name was bestowed on Cottle county, on Pease river. He has a large kindred, of various names, yet in the state.

DARNELL, Nicholas H., born in Tennessee in 1806—served in the Florida war—came to San Augustine, Texas, in 1838—in the Cherokee battles of 1839—served in congress from 1841 to 1845—was speaker of the house—to the convention of 1845 and chosen by that body to carry the authenticated constitution to President Polk in Washington city. He removed to Dallas about 1858—was a captain on the frontier in 1860—represented Dallas county in the legislature of 1859-60 and called sessions of 1861, at the time of secession—was colonel of the 16th cavalry in the Confederate army—served in the constitutional convention of 1875 from the district of Dallas, Tarrant and Ellis, with John Henry Brown from Dallas and J. W. Ferris from Ellis—also in the legislature of 1874-75 from Tarrant. He has ever stood as an honorable and patriotic man of good talent and fine practical judgment, and now resides in Fort Worth, seventy-five years old, feeble in health, respected as a patriarch who has been ever faithful to his country.

DE LEON, Don Martin, the founder of Victoria and De Leon's colony in 1824, under the colonization laws of Mexico, was a native of the Canary Islands, settling first in the state of Tamaulipas—a man of very stern character, but honorable principles. He died of cholera in 1834. His son, FERNANDO, was commissioner of the colony to issue titles—a man of integrity, who left Texas during the revolution, but returned in 1845 and died before the late war. SYLVESTER, another son, was alcalde, a brave and generous man, greatly esteemed by the Americans. One of Don Martin's daughters was the wife of Captain Placido Venibedes, a brave Indian fighter and strong friend of the Americans, who, with his brother-in-law, Sylvester De Leon, was murdered by Mexican robbers on the Nueces in 1837. Another was the wife of General Jose M. J. Carbajal, since long known as a general in the pronunciamentos and revolutions by the Liberal or Republican party in Northern Mexico. General Carbajal was educated by, and a protege of, the celebrated Alexander Campbell, of Bethany, West Virginia, in whose religious doctrines he was a strong believer. During the French intervention in Mexico, General Carbajal rendered signal service to his country against the invaders, mention of which is made in the memoir of General Lew Wallace, in this work.

DIMMITT, Captain Phillip, came from Kentucky in the early years of colonial Texas—was a merchant in San Antonio prior to the revolution—a captain in command of Goliad after its capture in October, 1835—figured as a trader on the Mexican border and in military expeditions. He acquired a large estate in lands, and died a prisoner in Matamoros in 1841, leaving a widow (a Mexican lady) and several children.

DUVAL, John C., one of the few prisoners who miraculously escaped from the Fannin massacre at Goliad in 1836. He is a man of education and literary

tastes and a fine surveyor. His brother, Captain Burr H. Duval, was murdered at the time of his escape. Another brother, Thomas H. Duval, was United States district judge of Texas from 1856 till his death in Austin in 1878. Their father, William P. Duval, was a native of Virginia—a member of congress from Kentucky, whence he was appointed governor of Florida by President Jackson, and finally died in Austin, Texas. John C. Duval is yet living, unmarried.

DARDEN, Stephen H., a native of Mississippi—served in the Texian army of 1836—in the legislature from Gonzales in 1853-55-57 and 1859—entered the Confederate army as captain in the 4th regiment in Virginia—was wounded and disabled—came home and served in the last term of the Confederate congress. From 1874 to 1880 he was comptroller of the state—declined a fourth re-election and now resides in Austin. He is annointed in the estimation of all who know him as an honest, brave, generous and kind-hearted man, of fine intelligence and clear head.

ELDRIDGE, Joseph C., came from Connecticut to Texas in 1837, with his brother, John C. Both filled several positions under the government and were esteemed valuable men wherever tried. Joseph C. was commissioner of Indian affairs and the head of the party in 1843 that advanced into the hostile country as peace-proposers, the incidents of which are given in the memorial of general H. P. Bee and referred to in the sketch of the Torrey brothers. After annexation he was appointed a paymaster in the United States navy, residing in Brooklyn, New York, and held that position till his death in 1880. They belonged to an ancient and well-known New England family.

FLACO, war chief of the Lipans, was one of the most remarkable Indians in our history. He was born a warrior and became a chief before arriving at manhood. The Lipans were kindred of the Mescaleros of Mexico and lived in that country more or less. After 1836 they chiefly lived in Southwest Texas, somewhat in union with the friendly Tancahuas. Their principal chief was Colonel Castro, who carried about his person a colonel's commission from President Sam Huston, and an older one as a brigadier-general in the Mexican army. He died about 1841, having led his band of scouts often with the whites. He was with Colnel John H. Moore in his expeditions in 1838-39 and 1840, in which young Flaco took part. Flaco was often, also, west with Hayes who held him in great esteem. In the Somervell expedition in 1842 he commanded a few of his warriors, acting with Hayes who commanded the advance. On the Rio Grande he dismissed all of his people, excepting an old deaf and dumb man, telling them to gather up plenty of Mexican horses and come home, which they did. He and this old man remained and came in with the party remaining with General Somervell, after the Mier separation. On leaving the Rio Grande, in conjunction with a man named Rivas and a Mexican he gathered and brought in sixty or seventy Mexican horses, on the principles of equal partnership. Arriving at San Antonio with the troops, these four encamped a few miles out with their animals. While asleep Flaco and his companion were murdered by the other two, who drove their horses into East Texas and Louisiana. Some days elapsed before the outrage became known—the disbanded volunteers had gone home—and the villains had gone east with none to pursue. It was generally the most dismal hour the country had ever seen, following the disaster at Mier, and, while indignation filled every breast, the murderers escaped unwhipped of justice. The Lipans could understand no explanation, and from that day to this, from their resumed haunts in Mexico, have been the enemies and the slayers of our frontier people, regardless of age or sex, though of late years rendered comparatively powerless. Flaco was then but twenty-four, over six feet in height, of manly form and the finest horseman I ever saw. But for that horrible crime, imagination can scarcely comprehend the anguish and the horrors, since experienced on that frontier, which would never have had existence. What became of the despicable wretches is not known.

FISHER, William H., from Richmond, Virginia, of good education, very tall and slender, came to Texas in 1834,—was in the Indian battle in the cedar brakes of the San Marcos, in April, 1835—a captain in the battle of San Jacinto—secretary of war in Houston's first term—a colonel in the Republican army of Mexico, in 1839-40—a captain in the Somervell expedition of 1842, and, after the separation of the command elected colonel of the three hundred who remained on the Rio Grande, fought the battle of Mier and became prisoners. He was a prisoner twenty-two months and released with the last of his comrades. He returned home in the winter of 1844-45, married a charming lady and died in Galveston in 1845. He was an accomplished gentleman.

FISHER, John, a brother of William S., settled in Gonzales in 1834—signed the declaration of independence and served in the army of 1836. His fate is unknown to the writer; but he was an educated, courageous and gentlemanly man.

FISHER, Samuel Rhoads, a native of Philadelphia, went in early life to St. Louis, Missouri, thence to Texas. He was a prominent man in Austin's colony, resident in Matagorda—signed the declaration of independence—secretary of the navy under President Houston and lost his life in a personal encounter in 1839.

HILL, George W., a man of fine ability, long resided at the frontier town of "Old Franklin," in Robertson county, and took an active part in the defense of the country. He served repeatedly in congress, was a member of President Houston's last cabinet and long in the state senate, always wielding an influence for the public good—a really valuable man in his day. Hill county was named for him. He died in the prime of life, before the late war, at his home, Spring Hill, in Navarro county.

HOOD, General John B., a native of Kentucky,

educated at the United States military academy—served in the army as a lieutenant and was stationed on the Texas frontier, where he established a stock farm or ranche and was greatly esteemed by the people. He claimed Texas as his home. He entered the Confederate army as colonel of the famed 4th Texas infantry in Virginia, and rose rapidly to be a brigadier, then major-general and lieutenant-general. He won the highest distinctions in the battles of Virginia—lost a leg at Chickamauga, and continued to ascend the ladder of fame till placed in chief command of the Army of the Tennessee, in place of Hon. Joseph E. Johnston. Then followed the campaign into Tennessee, with the sanguinary battle of Franklin, his defeat before Nashville and retreat. These events are matters for military criticism. But for undaunted spirit and personal heroism, by common consent, General Hood ranks second to no man in either army. His death in New Orleans, with that of his wife, leaving eleven little children, including three pairs of twins, called forth a burst of sympathy honorable to our country.

HELM, Major George, came from Kentucky to Texas, a passenger on the schooner, "Only Son," from New Orleans, landing in Matagorda bay in February, 1822. He selected land on the Colorado and was about returning for his family when he suddenly died. His family remained in Kentucky. One of his sons became governor of that state. Another is the Rev. Samuel Larue Helm, D. D., an eminent Baptist divine of Louisville.

HAWLEY, Rev. John L., came from Philadelphia to Southwest Texas in 1847, suffering with consumption. He was an accomplished scholar and captivating orator. He read law under Vice-President George M. Dallas and entered upon a splendid practice, but abandoned it to become a minister in the Presbyterian church. Neither the genial climate nor the gentlest care of newly made Texas friends afforded permanent relief, and he died in New Braunfels about 1850, deplored as a man of pure heart and remarkable talent. His widow and infant son, John Marshall Hawley, returned and took up their abode in Germantown, Pennsylvania.

JOHNSTON, General Albert Sidney. The life of this eminent man, in two large volumes, from the pen of his accomplished son, Colonel William Preston Johnston, has so recently been given to the public that we are content to say he was a Kentuckian, educated in the United States military academy at West Point, at the same time as several others who became distinguished on both sides in the late civil war. As a lieutenant in the United States army he served in the Black Hawk war with Jefferson Davis. He resigned in 1835-36—offered his sword and hand to Texas—became first adjutant-general in 1836, then commander-in-chief till the disbandment in 1837, secretary of war under President Lamar, serving in 1838-39 and 1840, was wounded in the Cherokee battles of 1839, commanded a Texas regiment in the beginning of the Mexican war in 1846, and, after its disbandment, served on the staff of General Taylor at

Monterey and Buena Vista. By President Polk he was re-appointed as a major and paymaster in the United States army, subsequently made colonel of one of the new cavalry regiments, commanded as brevet-brigadier-general the Utah expedition, winning distinction, and when the late war began, being in California, he resigned, joined the Confederacy and was appointed one of the full generals of its army, second only in rank to the highest. He organized the army at Bowling Green, Kentucky, retreated before Buel and fought the battle of Shiloh, April 6 and 7, 1862, where he was killed on the 6th, under circumstances illustrative of his chivalrous character. General Johnston ranks in our history, by the consent of eminent commanders on both sides of the struggle, as one of the ablest military chieftains yet produced in the United States. But he occupies a yet higher place in the hearts of the people, especially those of Texas, based upon his exalt d personal worth. No man who ever held an American commission, either in civil or military life, stood more spotless before the world. His name is ever spoken with respect, admiration and affection. His widow, a lady of rare excellence, still resides in California where the war of 1861 found her; but in every Texas household she has an abiding place.

JONES, William E., a lawyer and planter, with his parents, brothers and sisters, came from Georgia to Texas in 1839, chiefly settling in Gonzales county, though he subsequently resided in Seguin, New Braunfels, in the mountains of Kendall county, and died in Georgetown in 1871 or 1872, while judge of that district. He had served in the Georgia legislature and was editor of the Augusta *Chronicle and Sentinel*. He was elected to the Texas legislature in 1841 and again in 1842, but, in September of the latter year, was captured with the court and others to the number of about fifty-three, and carried to the City of Mexico. In 1843 he was released at the intercession of his old friend, General Waddy Thompson, then United States minister, and, on reaching home, again elected to congress. By that body, at the session of 1843-44, he was elected district judge and served by re-elections under the Republic and state some ten years. He returned to the bench in 1870 and died as stated. Under the Republic, as district judge, he was also a member of the supreme court. He opposed annexation to the United States in 1845 and secession from them in 1861, but ever retained the public confidence from the acknowledged sincerity of his character. He commanded a company throughout the war for the defence of the frontier on which he lived. He was a fine scholar and writer and an impressive orator, always conservative and logical. Of a large family of brothers and sisters, but one survives, Mrs David E. Smith, of Gonzales.

KLEBERG, Judge Robert, came from Germany to Austin county, Texas, in 1834, and was a soldier in the battle of San Jacinto, a man of fine mind and good education, ever esteemed as a worthy citizen. In 1846 he settled in DeWitt county, of which he was long chief justice and in which he still resides,

nearly eighty years of age. His sons, Marcellus E. Kleberg, of Galveston, served in the legislature of 1873, after graduating from Washington-Lee University, and Rudolph Kleberg, of Cuero, are both lawyers and young men of fine promise. The old patriarch has given all his children fine educational opportunities and may well feel, surrounded by a population holding him in the highest respect and esteem, that his half century of Texas life has not been in vain.

KERR, James, born in Kentucky, September 24, 1790, removed to Missouri in 1808, was sheriff, representative and senator, and came to Texas in February, 1825, settled as surveyor at Gonzales, laid off that town, was broken up by the Indians July 3, 1826, then settled on the Lavaca, surveying lands in the colonies of DeWitt and De Leon. He was in the convention of 1833, a soldier in 1835, member of the provisional government, elected to the convention but did not sign the declaration, because escaping with his family. He served in the congress of 1838-39 and held various public trusts. He was a man of superior practical talent and exercised great influence for good. He died December 23, 1850.

KENT, Andrew, came with his family, in 1828, from St. Charles county, Missouri, to what is Lavaca county, his head-right league being on the river of that name. He entered the Alamo, with Bonham, through leaden rain, there to die for Texas, for which Kent county perpetuates his name.

KARNES, Colonel Henry W., came to Texas from Tennessee in 1831, a brave, enterprising pioneer, won distinction in the storming of San Antonio, December 5 and 10, 1835, commanded the scouts on the retreat of General Houston, fighting the Mexican advance on the Navidad, was captain of cavalry at San Jacinto, commanded in several Indian battles, 1836 to 1840, was a prisoner in Matamoros in 1836, a prisoner among the Comanches in 1837 or 1838 and died while rapidly in rising fame, with the rank of colonel, in San Antonio, in December, 1840. Karnes county was named for him in 1853.

LINN, John J., the elder of four broters, (Charles, Henry and Edward), was born in Ireland about 1802 and brought up by his parents to New York in infancy. His parents, brothers, sisters and himself came from New York to Victoria, Texas, in 1830. The brothers were Mexican traders. Charles and Henry died in Mexico before the revolution, Edward at Goliad since the late war. John J., the only survivor of that once influential family has lived in Victoria fifty-one years. He was a soldier in 1835 and a member of the provisional council in 1835-36, a member of congress in both 1837-38 and 1838-39, long mayor of Victoria, a leading merchant for many years, and ever a man of integrity and influence. He married Miss Margaret Daniels, an accomplished young lady of New Orleans, who yet survives and beloved by all yet spared who knew her in those dismal days. His first child was born on the day of San Jacinto, under a friendly Mexican roof, but inside the enemy's lines, while he was a refuge from his young wife in the army. He was ever faithful to his country.

MILAM, Colonel Benjamin R., an unlettered native of Kentucky, was a volunteer in the patriot army of Mexico during the revolution against Spain, left the country in disgust when Iturbide was proclaimed emperor, entered Texas at an early day, obtained a colonial grant, was imprisoned in Mexico through jealousy of the Centralists in 1834-35, escaped in 1835, joined the army the night Goliad was captured, October 9, 1835, and on the fifth night of December led the storming columns into San Antonio. He gloriously fell on the eighth, two days before the surrender of the Mexicans, under General Martin Perfecto de Cos. Milam county preserves his name.

MENEFEE, William, came to Texas in the winter of 1829-30, from Tuscumbia, Alabama, though a native of East Tennessee. He was a substantial planter on the Colorado in what is now the upper part of Wharton county, a man of fair English education, of vast inteligence acquired by self-culture and a fine public speaker, a patriot by nature, inheritance and parental training, and a most valuable man in the public service. He served in the consultation of 1835, in the provisional council, signed the declaration of independence, served in the Texian congress throughout its existence and several times in the legislature, and died in Fayette county in 1876. He was one of a large kinship who came to Texas together, embracing, besides his own name, those of Southerland, White, Heard, Devers and Rogers, who settled in 1830, some on the Colorado, but chiefly on the Navidad, in what is now Jackson county, and became known as the "Alabama" settlement, to which reference is elsewhere made. Here I will say, once for all, that they were plain, practical, liberty-loving, honest Methodist people, with an injection of baptism through various marriages. A better average kindred, so numerous, never came to Texas, speaking as one who knew them in his youth and knows the survivors unto this day.

MENEFEE, John S., nephew of William and son of Thomas, (a plain farmer), a man of good education and fine mind, a soldier in 1835 and at San Jacinto, a true soldier, who fought under a sense of duty to his country, but, outside of war, was too tender hearted to shoot at a deer or turkey for food, without shutting his eyes and asking for forgiveness. In the great invasion of 1840, as one of three scouts, he became isolated and had a single handed combat with a warrior on the Arenoso, in Jackson county. He received seven arrows into his body, at last threw his empty pistol between his antagonist's eyes, hid under the creek bank, and, after a day of bleeding anguish, walked and crawled to the nearest ranche, bearing in his hands the seven arrows which he had pulled from his body and which he yet has in his Jackson county home. Otherwise he has been county clerk, county judge, a member of congress in 1839-40, and generally a benafactor to those among whom he has lived fifty-one years.

MOREHOUSE, General Edwin, a native of New York,

removed first for a number of years to Clarksville, Pike county, Missouri, to Texas in 1826, in 1835-36 brought out a battalion from New York, but landed too late to be in the battle of San Jacinto, though in hearing of the guns, commanded a regiment till the disbandment in May, 1837, served in the first senate of 1836-37, elected brigadier-general of militia in 1838-39, commanded a fruitless expedition up the Brazos in 1839, died in Houston in 1849. His brother, Dickerson B. Morehouse, of Galena, Illinois, was long a well-known steamboat captain on the Upper Mississippi.

MILLER, Dr. James B., a talented physician from Lexington, Kentucky, came to Texas before the revolution and was political chief of the Brazos before that event, a senator of the Republic and held various prominent offices. He was universally popular as a man of talent, honour and kindness of heart, and died at Richmond, on the Brazos, in 1854.

MOORE, Dr. Francis, jr., a native of Steuben county, New York, highly educated, a fine writer and geologist, who accidently lost an arm in his youth. From 1836-37 to about 1850 he was editor of the Houston *Telegraph*, senator from 1839-40 to 1841-42, long mayor of Houston, state geologist in 1859 and 1860, and died while on a visit in Philadelphia, in 1864. He was a fine orator, a sincere Presbyterian and one of the purest men in the country, in whose nature patriotism was a passion. His widow and children, at last accounts, resided in Philadelphia.

McKINNEY, Thomas F., a native of Kentucky, but came from Missouri via Santa Fe and Chihuahua to Texas in 1826, a valuable man of enterprise and public spirit and a true patriot. Of the commercial house of McKinney & Williams, at Velasco, when the revolution broke out, they made great advances and pecuniary sacrifices for the cause. From 1837 to 1849 they conducted a large house in Galveston, he serving in the first state senate, removed to Travis county in 1849, served in the legislature in 1857-58, invested largely in blooded stock, lost his fortune during the civil war and died in 1873, leaving a widow but no children. His memory is greatfully cherished by thousands all over Texas, who know of his honorable and useful identification with the country, in all of its trials, during his forty-eight years residence in it.

MURPHREE, David, a brave, generous and accomplished gentleman, came as a volunteer from Randolph, Tennessee, in 1835, a lieutenant in Captain Peacock's company, which served at San Antonio. As first lieutenant he commanded a company at San Jacinto, settled as a merchant at Victoria and resided there till he was brutally murdered in 1866, while on business in Missouri. He served in many frontier expeditions and was a major in the Somervell expedition in 1842. His only surviving child, James Owen Murphree, resides in DeWitt county. The other, Alexander, was killed in the battle of Mansfield.

MUNSON, Mordello S., born in Texas in 1825, an able lawyer, a soldier in 1840-41 and 1842 and in the Confederate army. He has been a prominent and useful member of the legislature from Brazoria, his life-long home.

MANCHACA, Antonio, a noble Mexican born in Santonio in 1800. A Texas soldier at San Jacinto and in many frontier engagements, an ardent patriot and ever true to the Americans. He died at the age of eighty.

MORGAN, General George W., a native of Ohio, came to Texas in 1836 as captain of a company of young volunteers and served till the disbandment in 1837. He afterwards returned to Ohio, became an eminent lawyer, legislator, member of congress and a Union general in the late war. He resides at Mount Vernon, Ohio, and is held in high esteem in Texas. One of his youthful soldiers of 1836, Mr. Robert M. Williams, died in Dallas about 1877.

MOORE, Colonel John H., resident in Fayette county, from 1826 to his death in 1881, fifty-five years; a noted Indian fighter, often commanding expeditions, as in 1835, 1837, 1838, 1839 and in 1840, invariably successful. Was colonel commanding in the first skirmish at Gonzales, September 28, 1835, and served at San Antonio immediately following. In October, 1840, he attacked and destroyed a Comanche village, near where the Texas and Pacific railroad now crosses the Colorado river, killing or capturing nearly all. In 1842 he commanded, as second in rank, in the pursuit of the Mexican General Woll, beyond San Antonio. He was a giant in size, and ever esteemed a bold and sagacious leader; but never held nor sought civil office.

MORGAN, James, came from North Carolina to Texas, in colonial days, settled at Morgan's Point, head of Galveston bay—was a prominent and honorable man many years, of fine intelligence and talent; held various responsible positions, and was a gentleman of the "old school." He became entirely blind a number of years before his death, but retained his hold on the popular heart till the last.

MERRIMAN, Francis H., a lawyer from Connecticut, came to Texas young, and long stood at the front at the bar of Galveston. He was often a member of the senate—one of nature's noblemen, a fine humorist, and, perhaps, more universally popular among acquaintances than any prominent man in the state. If he ever had an enemy the fact was unknown.

NEILL, General Andrew, a Scotchman by birth, came to Wellsburg, West Virginia, in his youth—became a lawyer—went to Mississippi, where he was probate judge. In 1836 he came to Texas as captain of a company of volunteers, under General Felix Huston, arriving just after the battle of San Jacinto; but was at once placed on special duty and rendered valuable service till the disbandment of the army in 1837. He then located as a lawyer, first at Gonzales and afterward at Seguin, where he resided from 1840 till about 1866, when he located in Galveston. Thence, about 1876, he removed to his present home in Austin. General Neill was long identified with the struggles of the Southwestern pioneers, often in battle with the Indians and Mexicans, and always in the front when danger was at hand. He acted with the greatest gallantry at Plum creek, August 12, 1840; at San Antonio, March 6, 1842, on the retreat of the Texians; in most of the events of that year of raids and fights; and in a bloody fight with the Indians in 1843, was severely wounded. On the eleventh of September, 1842, in San Antonio, with the judge, officers of the court and sundry lawyers and citizens, he was captured by the Mexican general, Adrian Woll, and carried into Mexico. His escape was remarkable. On this side of the Mexican lakes, at dusk, he slipped from the guard, and, during the night, waded and swam some miles into the city, arriving at dawn. Secreting himself, he soon beheld an Irishman, Sullivan by name, and a noble gentleman, to whom he made himself known. By that gentleman he was taken to his own house, cleanly shaven, newly clad and cared for. In due time, so complete was the disguise, he traveled to Vera Cruz in the same stage with the officer from whom he escaped, and duly reached home. He was commissioned brigadier-general by Governor Sam Houston, and resides in Austin, one of the honored survivors of 1836. General Neill married in 1844, Miss Agnes Brown, of Gonzales, a charming and accomplished lady, who died of yellow fever in Galveston, in 1867. He is blessed in a second union with Miss Jennie Chapman, a Virginia lady, beloved by a large circle of friends for those excellencies that adorn domestic and social life.

OUSBURY, Charles A., with his twin brother, John J., came from New York, in the Morehouse battalion in 1835-6, leaving their father clandestinely. He had already seen commercial service in China and at sea, but was still a youth. Arriving on the field of San Jacinto the day after the battle, he served as a guard over Santa Anna, and the Mexican prisoners, and remained in the army till 1837. His twin brother died in the autumn of 1836. In 1839 he was in both the battles with the Cherokee Indians and wounded. In 1840 he was in the battle of Plum Creek, and served otherwise on the frontier. From 1849 to 1872 he was, alternately, merchant and editor of the Bulletin, omitting the period of the war, at Indianola. Since the latter date, till 1881, he edited the same paper at Cuero. During the late war he served chiefly on the Rio Grande. He is a generous, noble-hearted man, well versed in, and proud of, his connection with Texas history.

ORR, Rev. Green, (whose twin brother, Washington, was a well-known Methodist preacher in Southeast Missouri), was a native of South Carolina, and a cousin of the late Governor James L. Orr. Of limited education he early became a Methodist preacher in Arkansas and Northeast Texas. From 1848 till his death in 1863, he resided in Indianola, and died while the Federal army occupied that place. His zeal in good works, in a mixed population—his sympathy with the distressed—with his purity and sincerity of character, made him a power for good among all classes. By old and young, black and white, native and foreign born, he was affectionately styled Father Orr, and, though circumscribed in the field of his usefulness, reverence for his memory abides in every heart. He was one of the best men that ever honored Texas in her primitive days.

PILLSBURY, Captain Timothy, a sea captain from Maine, came to Brazoria in the days of the Republic; a stalwart man with a wife and ten children. The people, sugar planters, slave-holders and all, liked the old salt from Maine. They sent him repeatedly to the Texian congress; made him county judge, and, when annexation was accomplished, the people of West Texas elected him to the United States congress in 1845 and again in 1847. He served four years, then moved to East Texas, where he died. One of his sons was the first mayor of New Orleans after reconstruction, who stopped public plunder and protected the people against organized wrong. Texas honors the name of Pillsbury.

POTTER, Robert, a very talented man and brilliant orator, a native of North Carolina, studied law, served two terms in congress from that state, and came to Texas before the revolution. He signed the declaration of independence, and served in the cabinet of President Burnet. In 1840 he was elected a senator from the Harrison or northeast district of the Republic, and was a leading member during the succeeding session, but was killed, the result of a local feud, in 1841. Potter county is named in his honor.

POTTER, Henry N., a lawyer of Galveston and once a representative in the Texas congress, was a native of Connecticut, educated in the state of New York, and came to Galveston in 1838. He died just after the late war.

POTTER, Mark Milton, a brother of the last named, was born in New York, educated at Marion College, near Palmyra, Missouri, and came to Galveston in his twenty-first year in 1840. He was an able and distinguished lawyer—served in the legislature in 1847-8, and from 1853 to his death during the war. was a member of the senate, one of the ablest, most laborious and upright men who ever sat in that body.

POTTER, Reuben M., a native of one of the Northern states, held several positions under the Republic of Texas, but is chiefly known as the author of the Hymn of the Alamo, and as a writer and poet. Being in Matamoros on the return of the Mexican army from Texas in 1836, he published in the Texas almanac of 1868 a graphic account of the siege and fall of the Alamo, embracing much data from Mexican sources, previously unknown in Texas—a valuable contribution to our history. He is believed to be living in New York.

PLACIDO, Captain, war chief of the Tancahua Indians; from boyhood to death a brave and true friend of the whites; a man of keen, native sense, and of inestimable service on the frontier from about 1834 to his death, and that of most of his tribe, at the hands of the Comanches and Kiowas in Fort Cobb, Indian territory, during the late war. With more or less of his warriors he was in countless expeditions with the whites against the hostile tribes, and in many engagements, always displaying the most fearless courage. He long lived near the settlements of the Guadalupe, La Vaca and Colorado, and was ever

ready to respond to the call of Burleson, Moore, Caldwell and other active leaders. Anecdotes innumerable illustrate his sagacity, fidelity and courage. He was tall, slender and lithe, a graceful rider, indulging always, unless in action, in dignified taciturity. In action his yell was eagle-like and his face aflame with fierce fury. His hatred of the Comanche, the immemorial enemy of his people, was intense, and for him he had no mercy. Men who sleep in their graves, if permitted to arise, could tell thousands of Texas-reared men and women how their infantile lives, directly and indirectly, were preserved by the watchfulness, the fidelity and the courage of this murdered son of the forest.

ROBERTSON, Colonel E. Sterling C., only son of Colonel Sterling C. Robertson, founder of Robertson's colony, came, when a boy twelve years of age, from Nashville, Tennessee, to Texas in 1832. His father had been educated in the Spanish language in Monterey. He rendered good service on the frontier; commanded a company in the Somervell expedition of 1842; filled various public positions, among them that of translator in the land office; member of the secession convention of 1861, and of the constitutional convention of 1875. He was, also, judge of Bell county, and brigadier-general of militia, by appointment of Governor Houston, and a Mason of high rank—also a member of the Methodist church. He founded the beautiful town of Salado, in Bell county, and chiefly originated and built up the college of that place. He served in various capacities in the late war, though in infirm health during its progress. He inherited a large and valuable landed estate, and died at Salado in 1879, leaving an ample fortune to his widow and twelve children.

ROMAN, Major Richard, a Kentuckian, came to Texas in the winter of 1835-6, as captain of a company which he commanded in the battle of San Jacinto, after which he was promoted to be a major in the army. He was, also, elected to the first congress from Victoria, and until annexation was almost continuously in the senate or house, a wise and upright legislator as he was a man. He filled other important trusts, was on the traveling board west of the Brazos, in 1840, to detect fraudulent land titles, and served, also, in the Federal (Revolutionary) army of Mexico, under Canales, in 1839. He was United States quartermaster in the Mexican war, and went to California in 1849. He filled various offices in that state, as senator and state treasurer; but of latter years was entirely deaf and lived in retirement. He died about 1877 or 1878. His memory in Texas is without blemish and fondly cherished by his surviving comrades.

SUTHERLAND, Captain George, (see Menefee), was one of the Alabama settlers that went on the Navidad in 1830—a stalwart man of six feet four and weighing nearly three hundred pounds, and married to Fanny, sister of Thomas and William Menefee. He was a captain before San Antonio in 1835, volunteered under Milam, to storm the place, and served until the surrender. On the first day at San Jacinto, his horse was killed under him. On the next day he went in on foot, and displayed a courage which was universal—epidemic, so to speak—on that glorious day. He served in the congress of 1837, was a man of superior mind, but very limited education. He died in 1853.

SUTHERLAND, William, a youthful son of Captain George, was a martyr of the Alamo—a promising boy, greatly beloved by the pioneers among whom his young life was given to his country and liberty.

SUTHERLAND, Mrs. Fanny, wife of Captain George and mother of William, known to us all in those primitive days, embodied all the excellencies of a true and patriotic farmer's wife, when danger lurked behind every tree. Beautiful and motherly, a fine housekeeper, pure as the snow of heaven, a thorough housewife, and devoutly trusting in the God she served, she went to her grave honored and revered.

SYLVESTER, Captain James A., a native of Baltimore and a printer. He came to Texas from Cincinnati, (really Covington, Kentucky, opposite Cincinnati), as a sergeant in a volunteer company, in the winter of 1836; was in the battle of San Jacinto, and, on the next day, April 22, 1836, captured and carried into camp Santa Anna. Four or five others were near by and went to him; but to him primarily and essentially is due the credit of the capture. He hastened back to Cincinnati, raised a company, and came back as its captain. He held various offices, and was in the Somervell expedition of 1842 to Mexico. In 1843 he settled in New Orleans and yet resides there, though always considering himself a quasi Texian.

STEWART, Dr. Charles B., an educated and high-toned gentleman from South Carolina, came to Texas about 1830, filled various offices in the revolution, as secretary of the governor, etc.; signed the declaration of independence; served in the convention of 1845, in the first state legislature, and at different times since down to the session of 1874-5. He is a man of literary taste, vast intelligence, a fine writer and has been a valuable citizen for more than fifty years. He has long resided at Danville, Montgomery county.

STAPP, Darwin M., came from Palmyra, Missouri, with his parents, five brothers and two sisters, in 1830, settling on the La Vaca river. His father, Elijah Stapp, signed the declaration of independence, and died in 1842. His elder brother, William P., was a Mier prisoner, and published the volume called the Prisoners of Perote. His youngest brother, Walter W., when a boy, served in the Somervell expedition of 1842; was sent to Indiana and Kentucky in 1843, and was there educated. He served in Marshall's Kentucky regiment in the Mexican war; became associate editor of the Frankfort, Kentucky, Yeoman, and died of yellow fever in South America, while filling the office of American consul. His brother, Oliver H., died of yellow fever at Bryan, in 1867. His brothers, Hugh S. and Archilles, and his sisters, (Mrs. Mary King and Mrs. Rebecca Steukes, of Southwest Texas), yet survive. His mother, a noble and loved woman, (nee Miss Shannon, of Kentucky), died in 1845. Darwin M. was a soldier in 1835-6 in the Grass fight and that of San Antonio; under Rusk

in 1836, at Plum creek in 1840, and on numerous frontier expeditions. He served in the legislature six years—1849 to 1855—and in the secession convention of 1861, and was collector of customs for the district of Saluria or Matagorda bay. He was a man of fine, native mind, fair education and noble heart, and died at his home in Victoria about 1877, leaving an honorable name to his posterity.

THURMOND, Major Alfred S., a Georgian, came to Texas a volunteer in 1837; served often on the frontier, distinguished for courage and tenacity of purpose; was in the battle of Salado, September 18, 1842; pursued a party of Indians on the San Antonio river, who had murdered Mr. and Mrs. Gilleland and carried off their little son (William M. Gilleland, now of Austin), and daughter. Thurmond and party recaptured the children. He was in the Somervell expedition, and adhered to the organization under Colonel William S. Fisher, which fought and surrendered at Mier. He became the interpreter for the prisoners, and was the only one allowed to witness the execution of the seventeen who drew black beans, and afterward of the yet baser murder of the heroic and stalwart Scot, Captain Ewen Cameron. When all but two beans were drawn, one was white, the other black, and these were to be drawn by Thurmond and James M. Ogden, a promising young lawyer, who had a widowed mother and dependent sisters at New Castle, Henry county, Kentucky. Thurmond, in keeping with his noble character, said: "Ogden, my people are well-to-do in Georgia. Your mother and sisters need your help; feel well of the beans; the black is slick, the white rough; draw it." Ogden replied "No; I dare not do so. I'll take the first my fingers touch." He did so and drew the last bean of death, and died as a resigned, Christian gentleman. Major Thurmond, after his release in 1844, served as sheriff of Victoria county; in the Confederate army as captain and major in New Mexico, Texas and Louisiana; in the legislature of 1866 and 1873, then residing at Rockport, on Arkansas bay. On the eighth of January 1876, with three families and others, he left Rockport, in a small vessel, for Tuxpan, Mexico. A storm prevailed during the succeeding night and day, and neither the vessel or passengers were ever heard of afterward. He left a widow, since deceased from a broken heart, and a little son, Dayton Thurmond, supposed to be in the care of his kindred. Notes of his eventful life, from his own pen, are in the hands of a lady in Dallas, known to him when she was a child, who, in due time, will prepare and publish them.

TORREY, John F., David S., Thomas S., and James, four brothers, from Ashford, Connecticut, came to Houston in 1836-7; saw much service on the Indian frontier; kept Torrey's trading house on the Tehuacano, east of where Waco is. Thomas was one of the trio, with Joseph C. Eldridge and H. P. Bee, in the thrilling expedition of 1843, described in the memoir of General Bee. He died the same year pending a council with Indians, in connection with that expedition, on Village creek, now in Tarrant county. James, a noble and gallant young man, was one of the seventeen decimated Mier prisoners in the same year. David S. was killed by the Indians in 1850. In later years John F. built and owned woolen mills at New Braunfels, attended with great prosperity till dual floods swept away his possessions. He now resides on his farm, covering Comanche Peak, in Hood county. There were other brothers, unknown to the writer. All were honorable and useful men.

USHER, Patrick, came from North Carolina, a young man and lawyer, to what became Jackson county, in 1834. He was a man of fine mind and spotless character. He was the first revolutionary judge of his county; a splendid soldier; again judge for several years; twice a member of congress in 1840 and 1841, and, in 1842, volunteered in the Somervell expedition to Mexico, which resulted in the sanguinary battle of Mier, where he and his comrades became prisoners. In the barbarous bean drawing, at the hacienda of Salado, in the state of San Luis, Patosi, he drew a white bean and escaped slaughter, but died during the next year, as a Mier prisoner, in the castle of Perote. He never married nor had a relative in Texas, but his memory and noble character are cherished by all who knew him.

VAN NESS, Cornelius, a native of Vermont, whose father, William P. Van Ness, was governor of that state; a member of congress and United States minister to Spain, Cornelius being the secretary of legation, where he became a Spanish scholar. He came to San Antonio, Texas, in 1836, and was a member of congress in 1837-8-9-40-41 and 1842; but was accidently killed in the spring of the latter year by the discharge of a gun hung to the pommel of a saddle on a "pitching" horse, in the streets of San Antonio. He was an able lawyer, a towering orator and a patriot of the highest type, and his death was deplored as a great loss to the country. He was about thirty, and seemed to have as brilliant a future as any young man in Texas.

VAN NESS, George, a younger brother of Cornelius, an adventurous young man of commercial pursuits, a prisoner in the ill-fated Santa Fe expedition. Released, he was a soldier in the autumn of the same year, (1842,) and afterwards in the Mexican war. Unambitious, he was a private citizen and a private soldier, loved by his fellows for his intelligence, his courage and his noble heart. [These two Green mountain boys, honored all over Texas, were supplemented from the same state in the persons of young Temple, son of an ex-member of congress from Vermont, who fought with us in 1842, and the lamented James Denison, first of Matagorda and last of San Antonio, besides Judge Joel Miner, deceased, of Austin, Rev. Caleb S. Ives, of Matagorda, and David Ives, his brother, a surveyor of Lavaca county, besides Martin Carroll Wing, elsewhere mentioned in alphabetical order.]

WITT, Captain Preston, (twin brother to Presley,) with several brothers, came to Dallas county, from Green county, Illinois, in 1843-44. He commanded a company from Dallas and surrrounding counties in Hayes' 2d regiment in the Mexican war, serving between Vera Cruz and the City of Mexico, and was in numerous engagements. In pursuit of a band of Indians from Dallas county, in what is now Wise county, he had a hand to hand fight with a powerful chief and slew him with his Bowie knife. He was a peaceable and every way worthy citizen and died in Dallas county in 1877.

WHARTON, William H. and John A., young lawyers of splendid talents and devoted brothers, came from Tennessee to Texas about 1825-26. William H. married Sarah A., the only daughter of Mr. Jared W. Groce, a planter on the Brazos, about 1827. On a visit to Nashville, Tennessee, their only child was born in that place. The child, John A. Wharton, jr., grew to manhood, was educated at the University of South Carolina, married a daughter of Governor Johnson of that state, and became by promotions from a captaincy, a major-general in the Confederate army, to die at the close of the war by an unfortunate collision, deplored by the people and thousands of mutual friends. William H. Wharton was an orator of the style of William C. Preston. He was in the battle of Velasco in 1832, president of the provincial convention in 1833, a member of congress at the sessions of 1836-39, lamented as one of the most brilliant stars in the galaxy that shed lustre on Texas in that era of intellectual giants and spotless patriots. The name, in lineage, is extinct, neither brother having a descendant to transmit it; but it is emblazoned on the pages of our history and perpetuated in the name of Wharton county, bestowed in their joint memory. The widow and only child of General John A. Wharton, the Confederate, both died since the war, leaving the name in Texas, as stated, extinct. A zealous advocate of war in 1835, with Austin and Archer a commissioner to the United State in 1836, a senator in the first congress, first minister to the United States, and died by the accidental discharge of his own pistol while a member of the senate in 1839. John A. Wharton, who never married, was an orator of a different style, dealing in burning eloquence, sharpened by incisive sarcasm. He served in the army in 1835 and 1836, and was adjutant-general at San Jacinto, a Harry Hotspur in action, his clarion voice calling upon others to follow and his flaming face bidding his comrades on to glory. He represented the people in the consultation of 1835, signed the declaration of independence, served in congress and died in 1838.

WING, Martin Carroll, a native and printer of Vermont, as brave and generous a man as ever shouldered a musket for Texas, came from New York in the Morehouse expedition in the winter of 1835-36, in the same brig with the (now) distinguished General William H. Loring, first of the Texian, next of the United States, then of the Confederate and lastly of the Egyptian army, ex-Governor Peter H. Bell, Colonel Charles de Morse, Charles A. Ogsbury, (and his deceased brother, John J. Ogsbury, who died in 1836 a Texas boy soldier), the deceased Judge James C. Allan, Louis P. Cooke, afterwards secretary of the Texian navy, and others who became distinguished. They were imprisoned in the West Indies as pirates,

www.ingramcontent.com/pod-product-compliance
Lightning Source LLC
Chambersburg PA
CBHW031822090426
42739CB00008B/1375